A Prophetic Instructional Manual

A guide to advance you in ministry

CONTENTS

A Fivefold Training Ministry Curriculum

SYLLABUS

1. **Dreams and Visions:**

   Developing revelation, dreams & visions
   Dreams & visions for personal communication
   A commission from God
   Correction & Reproof
   Instruction for inner healing

2. **Revelation for dreams & visions for the church:**

   Interpretation for others
   Spiritual revelation & Discernment
   Interpreting Symbols for dreams & visions
   God's order for church growth

3. **Birthing the Prophet:**

   The awakening of the prophetic office
   Humility & character is a pre-requisite
   First steps in prophecy
   A prophetic crawl or a prophetic walk
   The office of the prophet

4. **Advance prophetic education/fulfilling a mandate:**

   Introduction to prophetic intercession
   Spiritual mantles ~ and the treatment
   Mentorship ~ the right way
   Prophetic assessment

Chapter 1

Developing Revelations in Dreams & Visions

The basis of dreams & visions

In this chapter we will be learning about how God speaks to a prophet / prophetic person through dreams and visions, there are times when life's daily activities prevent us from taking adequate time to bask in God's presence so he can speak to us. So in turn, when our total being is at rest and our spirit is quieted. God will wait until we are sleep to speak to us. In light of the fact that our father speaks to us while we are in a state of rest, we must understand that our spirit man never sleeps.

God frequently makes use of dreams and visions to communicate his will to man in the bible there are many examples we will view to see how God spoke to his people. Among several topics in the church, dreams remain the most controversial. There are some who say "I never dream" or others say, "I don't pay attention to my dreams" I have been dreaming all my life and they don't mean anything. Although these things may be true, the way the Lord deals with others in the spirit presses them to meditate on their dreams.

So what do you think? Should we ignore our dreams and just take them as junk mail and put them in the recycle bin. I believe God gives us that answer in Joel 2:28-29 and Acts 2:16-20 says, But this is that which was spoken by the prophet Joel, And it shall come to pass in the last days, saith God, I will pour out my spirit upon all flesh: and your sons and your daughters shall prophesy and your young men shall see visions and your old men shall dream dreams: and on my servants and on my handmaidens I will pour out in those days of my spirit; and they shall prophesy : and I will shew wonders in heaven above, and signs in the earth beneath.

How to remember what God is speaking to you

The first way to begin this process is to start a prayer journal. Record the time date, location and significant events in your life. In your prayer time with the Lord take your journal with you to write down what the Holy Spirit might say to you. Also include feelings, impressions, tastes or smells, if it has colors, numbers, and people or names. If someone in the dream reminds you of someone you know, These are important clues. After this note the interpretation you think the dream may possibly have, and learn to ask the Holy Spirit for interpretation of what you saw, and when he answers trust him. Many times you will not receive interpretation right away but it will unfold for you if you continue to journal.

There are several ways the Lord will speak to you but first you must learn how to hear Gods voice.

1. Dreams
2. Visions
3. Journaling
4. Speaking in tongues
5. Impression / Feeling
6. Prophecy

Understanding dreams

Looking at dream interpretation in general it is important to know that not every symbol will have the same interpretation for every person what a father or a spouse may mean in one persons dream, may represent something totally different for another person. God has uniquely made us different so ask the Holy Spirit for revelation and write down what you receive in your journal. Dreams can tell you a lot about a person it can tell you what is in their heart and what the Lord is doing in their life. When you receive revelation for others, don't just give interpretation use this opportunity to minister to the person.

This is what the lord gives revelation for the use of ministry and encouragement.
Take the revelation the Lord gives you and add encouragement and counseling. To give the person faith and hope in the Lord God. As you use the gifts in you
You will be sharpened, a valuable tool in the hands of the master and a treasure in his eyes.

The most important key to correct dream interpretation is this; a dream usually addresses the circumstances of one's life as it presently exits. Although some dreams are prophetic in dealing with future events, most dreams are relevant to whatever is going on in the dreamer's life at the time of the dream

Another key factor in a dream may refer to the dreamers past. In this case there is usually something in the dream that will point to past events {a former residence, grandparents, old relationships, etc.} dreaming of one's own back yard almost always refers to someone's past.

Before you are able to interpret a dream for another person you must have some information about them. While some symbols are common amongst many people you must first learn what the relationship is with the person and the characters in the dream. You will need to know what the places and objects and scenes meant to them personally and most important you need to know if they are born again by the spirit of God. If you are to interpret by the spirit and by the word of God.

Keep in mind that in interpretation of symbols in dreams also depends on the culture and upbringing of the person. The Lord used a table cloth of unclean animals to get peter's attention. Peter was Jewish so the symbols in his dream were very clear to him. "It yelled, uncommon and unclean" this was a representation of the gentiles, (Acts 10:9-20) so the Lord will use symbols that are common to you and your culture to speak to your spirit.

As a child of God most symbols for prophetic dreams will come from the word of God. Because this is one culture we all belong to as the Body of Christ. So it is important to know your scriptures and get answers from the word of God.

What type of information does dreams supply

Although dreams may cover almost any situation that one may encounter in life, there are several areas in which God often deals with us through dreams. As Elihu said when he said to Job about dealing with man through dreams. "Lo all these things worketh God often times with man, to bring back his soul from the pit to be enlighten with the light of the living. {Job 33: 29, 30}.

Personal Information

If Pilate had listened to his wife's warning, would his circumstance have changed? The dream was from the angel of the Lord. Or did God know he would disobey the warning. {Matt 27: 19} When he was set down on the judgment seat, his wife said unto him saying, Have thou nothing to do with that just man, for I have suffered many things this day in a dream because of him. The warning came, and was given, shows how we comprehended what we hear from God. Sometimes God will send a warning through a dream before we are tested, have tribulation, and temptation.

Self-examination

When seeking direction from God for personal holiness, to clean, purify and sanctify. Even when God himself is bring up some things out of your soul to deliver you. {II Cor: 13:5} examine yourselves, weather ye be in faith; prove your own selves. Know ye not your own selves, how that Jesus Christ that is in you except ye be reprobates. When taking self-examination into consideration one might think of some examples such as smoking cigarettes in a dream as an indication of one walking in pride or bitterness, unforgiveness. Or smoking cigars which usually speak of arrogance. Likewise nudity may mean walking in the flesh or being without God's covering {or something being exposed}.God will always deal with you first before he can deal with you about anyone else so pay close attention.

With the prophetic we must understand the ways God will speak to us, and when novice or infantile you must learn the pattern of your dream cycle at each level. In a dream you must ask God who is this for me, the person or the church universal. Or is it for what is coming to the world. Will get to the deeper levels in another chapter.

Personal guidance and direction

Concerning ones marriage, career, location, or ministry. {Matt 1:20} "But while Joseph thought on these things, behold an angel of the Lord appeared unto him in a dream, saying Joseph, thou son of David, fear not to take unto thee Mary: for that which is conceived in her is of the Holy Ghost".

Personal Warnings

Concerning natural provisions as well as employment, marriage, financial decisions. {Matt 2:22} But when Joseph heard that Archelaus did reign in Judea in the room of his father King Herod, he was afraid to go thither, notwithstanding being warned of God in a dream"

Direction in ministry

{Acts 16:9} And a vision appeared to Paul in the night; there stood a man of Macedonia and prayed him saying come into Macedonia, and help us.

Messages for churches:

If you are active in ministry {Pastor, Evangelizing, or traveling etc.) oftentimes God will give you a message for his people through dreams. {Num 12:6) and he said hear now my words: if there be a prophet among you I the Lord will make myself known unto him in a vision, and will speak unto him in a dream.

Truth

{John 16:13} When the spirit of truth is come he will guide you into all truth, this include doctrines or traditions that have been taught by man, he will also give answer to questions you have been asking through a dream.

Strong self-will or desires

{Jer 29:8} For thus says, the Lord of hosts, the God of Israel, let not your prophets and your diviners, that be in the midst of you deceive you neither harken to your dreams which ye caused to be dreamed.

{Ezek 13:1, 2} Woe unto the foolish prophets that follow their own spirit, and have seen nothing. The novice prophet must seek Godly council from other seasoned prophets so they don't have pitfalls in this area. The human soul is capable of voicing thoughts, ideas, and inspirations out of the unsanctified portion of our emotions, we must be careful not to trust how we feel about things, our emotions can guide us wrongly. The human inspirations are not necessarily born of God. As Ezekiel said, they are prophecies" out of their own hearts,

Tools for understanding dreams

Dreams originate from three different sources, God our soul, and demons. The first element in interpreting dreams is to properly determine where the dream came from. If it is from God we need to understand it and incorporate the directions and information it reveals into our actions. If it is from our soul, we need to recognize the problem, and with prayer, deal with it accordingly. And finally if it is from a demon, we need to pray for deliverance from this influence and over the room and area that has been occupied to rid ourselves of this influence.

One of the most difficult problems we may encounter with dream interpretation is determining whether the person or people, represent themselves another person, or something else{ personality, character, saved or unsaved etc.} for instance a pastors wife may represent the church, or a man's wife represent his job. And of course she can simply represent herself.

If God wants to show us another person's state, he may put us in the persons place {. Or we may stand proxy} so that we can see and feel things and have a deeper discernment about what it is he is saying about them. This can be through thoughts actions, speaking and feelings.

Nightmares demonic and X-rated dreams {one who needs deliverance} indicates demonic presence, and allowing you to know where the deliverance is needed. Whether it is a demon, allowed through opened doors, inherited curses, or self-inflicted bondage, a child or someone who has a spirit of fear may wake up crying because a spirit has given him/her a bad dream. Sometimes the spirit lives in the room instead of the person. {Psalm 19:9} The fear of the Lord is clean enduring forever; the judgments of the Lord are true and righteous altogether.

There are times in our lives that we are not paying attention to what God is saying to us. When God seems to magnify things in our dreams, He is trying to get our attention of the things that we have not took notice to. Repetitive dreams are very important. When God continually talks to you or reminds you of something it is important {Job: 33:14, 15} for God speaketh once yea twice, yet man perceiveth it not. In a dream, in a vision of the night, when deep sleep falleth upon men. In slumbering upon the bed.

Night visions are usually brief, direct communication from God. They often contain instructions, warnings and encouragement. Unlike dreams {parables} they seldom need interpretation. See {Acts 16:9, 10- 18: 9, 10

Definitions

Dreams: dreams are the vehicle of communication from God to the vessel. From the spirit realm to the natural realm where the dreamer can communicate information God has given them. Dreams visually communicate a way of seeing things in the dreamer's natural environment.

Prophetic Dream: One that has predictive and revelatory implications. Prophetic dreams impart visions, deposits God's word and/or establishes truth. These dreams are used to determine what God is doing in the spirit realm that has not yet appeared in the natural.

Prophetic Dreams differ from visions. Although both are predictive and revelatory in nature. A prophetic dream is communicated in a language of symbolism that is recognized to the dreamer's sphere of life. Also a prophetic dream is when God is implanting a message in the dreamer's heart and mind.

Vision: seeing the events or manifestation of the supernatural world with awakened and elevated natural faculties {Gen 15:1, Isa 1:1, Dan 9:23} these passages reference a vivid apparition not a dream.

Visions & Dreams to a Prophet

The customary way the Lord awakens the spirit of prophet's to let them know they are ordained to fill the office. {Num 12:6} And he said, Hear now my words if there be a prophet among you, I the Lord will make myself known unto him in a vision and speak unto him in a dream.

Without these, the prophet ceases to be a prophet. You cannot be a prophet without God giving you dreams and showing you visions. At the same time it does not mean that you are a prophet just because you have dreams and visions. {Joel 2; 28 and Acts 2:17} we will talk about this later in greater detail.

In Chapter 8 of Amos there was a vision of the summer fruit. It is here that you see God has given Amos a vision. And then asks him what it was he had seen. Here he had to understand the symbolization the Lord was giving to him. Summer fruit came at the end of the year meaning a divine season. It could not come forth during the winter, spring, or fall seasons; it could not survive the climate. We also know that through visions is how God spoke to the prophets Jeremiah, Ezekiel and Isaiah.

Simple/symbolic message dreams apparently do not need to be interpreted. This is what I call literal face value dreams. As I always say it is what it is. Everything in a dream can happen just as you see it. But always consider whether a dream is literal. Simple/symbolic dreams have symbols clear enough for the dreamer or others interpreting the dream to understand. The objects, people colors and numbers, even ones actions are symbolic. The first scene in a sequence will usually provide the setting to give the subject and thus enables everyone to properly apply the dream, scene chances are usually progressive, and like a two or three act play, moves the plot forward with each scene containing additional information. Each symbol must be placed in its proper setting before its meaning will be clear.

Complex/Symbolic dreams require the interpretative skill of someone who has experience or has an unusual ability in interpretation { Daniel 2: 3, 16} Daniel was a Seer/prophet God gave divine revelation to interpret dreams, but even Daniel had interpretations with symbols that were so complex that he had to seek divine intervention in order to interpret. In Daniel Ch 8, we see God deals with and gave Daniel visions and we see Daniel receiving the interpretation for them through this God is revealing his will to Daniel.

Chapter 2

Revelation for dreams and visions for the church
Interpretation for others

In this chapter we will first learn how to interpret and judge your own revelation you receive from God. We have gone over the three different sources dreams originate from. Now we are going to understand how to interpret for ourselves, this is what we must understand first in order to judge revelation for others. Consider a time in our spiritual walk we are not sure of what we receive is coming from God. It is at this time we need to be sure if we have missed it or not. Just as we need to walk in the spirit (with our natural feet) so we should do so while we are in the spiritual realm in our dream state. (1 John 4; 1) says; beloved believe not every spirit but try the spirit whether they are of God. So how do we come to the place of knowing that the revelation you are receiving is from the Lord. And for some, being the watchman on the wall in the local church how do you judge the revelation for others.

Sometimes we can get revelation from God about something but receive the wrong interpretation about what God has given us. So what comes out is not an accurate representation of what God has said. This often takes place in those who are young (novice) in their prophetic walk this is often a case of immaturity and lack of the knowledge of the word. Hebrews 5:14 says; but strong meat belongeth to them that are of full age, even those who by reason of use have their senses exercised to discern both good and evil. Our capacity to feast on deeper knowledge of God (Strong meat) is determined by our spiritual growth at times we want to be invited to God's banquet before we are spiritually capable to digest it. As you grow in the Lord spiritually and walk in what you have learned your capacity to understand the more you will grow to the next level of maturation. This happens often in dream interpretation and most time we think if I am receiving revelation I must be mature to receive it. Not always true, first we must have a conducive prayer life and divine connection with the father. And then in a place to allow the Holy Spirit to purify our soul realm. Lining up with God's word as he transform our hearts and minds.

We can become deceived if we are not true with ourselves, we need to get in the word of God to first let it purify us. What we have to understand is our soul can make us think and feel things that are not in the will of God. We will be visiting both Daniel and Joseph and some of the prophets to get us to understand how to receive proper revelation from God. As it was said in the last chapter "it is what it is" "What you see, is what it is" face value. The difference between simple and complex symbolic dreams. A prophet or prophetic person can and will receive a revelation from God but not have the wisdom to interpret the symbols correctly the stage of this realm is just like when the gift of prophecy is being awakened in the prophetic person they are novice and all they do is prophesy all the time. In the prophetic sometimes God will put the gift on the shelf so to speak, so the prophet can understand there is more to being a mouth piece and prophesying breakfast, lunch and dinner. God gives us balance and gives wisdom and understanding if we ask him for it he will give wisdom to us liberally.

1 Kings 3:9 says; give therefore thy servant and understanding heart to judge thy people that I may discern between good and bad; Solomon asked God for wisdom when given a chance to have everything in the world, Solomon asked God for wisdom and an understanding heart in order to lead well and make right decisions. James 1:5 says if any of you lack wisdom, let him ask of God, that giveth to all liberally, and unbraided not, and it shall be given him. The key to this stage is asking God in prayer for wisdom and understanding. Wisdom from God is different than knowledge from a book. For example: I have a spiritual daughter that was novice in her gifting; she brought me a prophetic dream she had and with no understanding. The dream was she had a dream that she was telling someone she had a dream that her leaders had died and they were preparing for their funeral. She didn't see her leaders, or anyone else talking about their death. She was telling someone about their death and in a comment to the person she felt the loss of them and said she was going to miss their hugs and embrace. The dream went on further with me and others in a room so to speak and I was walking back and forth as she told me of her leaders passing.

And my response to her was its better that everyone dies because of the hour we are entering. For the time we are living in and where God was about to take his people. She woke up frantic and with a feeling of loss.
(Interpretation)

This dream is a twofold dream, God was telling the novice prophet it is time for some things in your life to die. This was not just about her but the dispensation of time we are entering for the body of Christ. If we want to connect/relate with Jesus Christ in his resurrection then we must really die to our flesh. God was allowing her to understand that he was doing some crucifying in her life first and then in others. Death in a dream symbolizes death to the flesh sometimes or emotions, or yielding your members unto God. Can we discern this when it appears in our dream state, can we make the difference between what is literal or what is complex symbolic?

Another dream a man of God had and didn't understand what the Lord was saying to him and this person is not a prophet but he is a Pastor. The dream: there was a funeral of someone the man had went to school with the person had died. The man of God and I went to this funeral, when it was time to view the body I recognized some people from church and began to converse with them. The man then went to view the body of the young lady. As he looked in the casket the young lady was alive, and trying to pull him in with her, he was struggling to get away from her. He looked around for me and others. No one seem to notice or help him. He woke from the dream.

(Interpretation)
In this dream God uses someone the man went to school with (his past, learning) and for it to be a female(men must get in touch with their emotions, heart issues) God allowing the lady to be alive in the casket and pulling him in with her spoke to the man of God's emotions and heart issues. And how his flesh was pulling him into places of keeping something's alive. God was trying to get him to yield to him. God was showing this Man of God death had to come of something's in him, and he needed to yield his member unto him.

Spiritual revelation & discernment

How to discern what the Lord is saying in the spirit and share it with others

Prophetic discernment: The ability of the prophet to detect manifestations, influences and apparitions or psycho-emotional conditions normally unseen or overlooked by non-prophetic types. Prophetic discernment is a cultivated gift that relies on experience, exposure to a wide range of prophetic ministry 1 Cor 12:10; one of the gifts of the spirit it apparently refers to the God giving ability to tell whether a prophetic speech came from God's spirit or from another source opposed to God. 1 John 4: 1-6; Hebrew 5:14.

Prophetic Instincts: Special faculties inherent in certain people where they sense, perceive and can identify what is happening behind the veil of this world. This faculty is available to all who have the Holy Spirit. Along with sensing the events, those that have this faculty understand its prophetic fraction, objectives and manifestations. These can also discern weather this event or action is or not of God. Also sensing the presence of a prophet's spirit in a person, or recognizing the shifts of the Lord from one stream of office to the other.

Prophetic drama: The delivery of prophesy whereby the prophet acts out the message this action of the prophet serves to allow God to issue his word to the prophet regardless were it is targeted to be fulfilled. A biblical case of this action is seen in the ministry of the prophet Ezekiel 4:4-6; were God called Ezekiel to enact the coming siege and fall of Jerusalem before it actually happened. He was instructed to lie on his left side for 390 days, and then lay on his right side for 40 days.

Prophetic sensations: the term for the diverse physical and physiological experiences felt by the prophet in preparation for duty. These sensations were felt by Jeremiah the prophet and it touched his human emotions, feelings, and discomforts. They include the weighty hand of the Lord resting upon them uncomfortably until a prophetic task is complete.

Our scripture reference for this chapter are Hebrews 5:11-14; 1 John 4: 1-6; Jude 1:17-23 the prophet in this section that we will use is Daniel, means (dan'yel) personal name meaning God is Judge, or God's Judge. Daniel was a high government official during the reins of Cyrus he also was famous with wisdom and righteousness. Daniel had outstanding physical attraction he demonstrated at an early age, propensities of knowledge, wisdom and leadership. In addition to his wisdom, he was skilled in dream interpretation. He was not classified as a prophet, but his interpretation skills makes him one. The prophecy of Daniel is the first great book of apocalyptic literature in the bible. The Greek word apocalypses, from which comes the English "apocalypse" means an unveiling, a disclosing or a revelation. Though all scripture is revelation from God, certain portions are unique in the form by which their revelation was given in the means by which they were transmitted. Apocalyptic literature in the bible has several characteristics: (1.) in apocalyptic literature a person who received God's truths in visions recorded what he saw. (2.) It makes extensive use of symbols or signs. (3.) Such literature nominally gives revelation concerning God's plan for the future of his people. Daniel had been the interpreter of two dreams of king Nebuchadnezzar chaps2, 4.

Symbols for dream interpretation

We are going to go into symbol and parable interpretation, remember every symbol may be a different representation for different people. What you must ask yourself what this symbol represents to me think about the natural inclination. What are the person's personality, character and life style?

1. *Age: In prophetics references to age carry two meanings. (1.) The period of time in which prophetic revelation being conveyed is set within. (2.) The number of years a person, place or thing has been alive or in existence. (B.) The degree of seasoning and object has reached to attain maturity.*
2. *Ancestral: that which pertains to a family linage genealogy. Prophetically this word is important in explaining the supernatural resources bestowed by the almighty but perverted by the demonic spirits that infiltrate and contaminate a family line. (Familiar spirits, ancestral spirits, and generation spirits).*
3. *Angel: a heavenly/spiritual being, divine messenger, sent as an agent, ambassador or emissary to conduct business on behalf of God in the affairs of men.*

4. *Angel of the seven churches: the seven angels to whom the apocalypse, received by the Apostle John was addressed. Angels were addressed because of the church's supernatural status and consequent need for supernatural power and redress in the earth. The angels not unlike Michael's assignment over the nation of Israel, are assigned by the Lord Jesus Christ to cover minister to and mediate on behalf as literal partners with the church's earthly leadership in its establishment and growth in the earth.*

5. *Apocalypse: (A) Revelation. (B) A term used for the last day events predicted or experienced on Earth according to the Bible. These are generally of a doomsday, last days, or cataclysmic nature. Revelations of this sort tend to permeate apostolic doctrine, which emphasizes finalization, transition, and renewal.*

6. *Baby: in prophetic dreams, a baby signifies the immature, the new, and unseasoned. It also reflects the start of something recently born or brought into existence. A baby indicates promise, male babies speak to the seeds, being sperm bearing, that when planted in the Earth become trees. Trees in this content represent nations. Female babies speak to fruit being the product of seed planted and grown and also the outcome of handling God's assignment as promised.*

7. *Backwards, back, or going back: (A) Back, departure, rejection, or refusal (B) the back speaks to negation or completion (C) Backward; the Bible uses this term, to describe apostasy and its results. God classifies people as having gone backward when they return to their old ways and choose their former paths and resources in life. Today we categorize this as backsliding.*

8. *Bankruptcy: the state or condition of being financially, morally, ethically, physically, or spiritually destitute. Without funds, character, soul, emotional response, or sensitivity; spiritual void of all that makes life worth living and prosperous.*

9. *Barrenness: Barrenness is the absence of fruitfulness in one's efforts or the inability to produce profitable fruit.*

10. *Bath, or Bathing or Bathroom: (A) Bath-in dream language speaks to washing away previous experiences, contamination, or flesh in preparation for a new day, change, or upgrade in lifestyle. (B) Bathing-the process whereby one takes away the old influences and their effects and prepares to enter the new. Bath and bathing both infer a transition from one act of service to another.*

11. *Bed or bedroom: A place of secrecy, rest, and intimacy. The center of the most private affairs and their causes to be executed. That which is attached to the state of the body and its spiritual and emotional needs. The sanctuary of psycho-emotional activity, desires, and fulfillment.*

12. *Birthing forth: the prophet or prophetic vessel, once impregnated in the spirit with the word of the Lord, can find his or her experience something akin to the gestation of a woman with child over the time it takes for the word to ripen and be mature enough to come forth. This can resemble the physical sensation and labor contractions of a woman. Jeremiah spoke of these physical sensations.*

13. *Black: A color that refers to calamity, sin, darkness, and sorrow. It also speaks of worldliness.*

14. *Blue-: A color that symbolizes spiritual dominance and heaven bestowed ruler ship; it also signifies unimpeded growth, unlimited potential and indomitable opportunity. Blue signified God's appearance and also symbolizes perpetuity of eternal government.*

15. *Bridge: A symbol of transition. In particular, transitions over the high grounds of life. Bridges can symbolize difficult life changes and rites of passage. Prophetically, bridges exemplify the arc over waters, troubled or serene, depending upon the issues causing the symbolism of the bridge. They signify external and apparent transitions.*

16. *Cloud: a prophetic symbol of celestial spirits and angels; spiritual vehicles upon which or within the heavenly citizens' ride.*

17. *Clocks and time: in prophetic dreams, clocks represent the Lord's revelation of His impending times and seasons as they pertain to shifts in His activities in the Earth. The time on a prophetic clock can appear as seconds, minutes, and hours. It takes prophetic revelation to determine if these in fact apply to days, weeks, months and years.*

18. *Dirt: Depending upon its condition, dirt in prophetic encounters, visions, and dreams can be a positive symbol. It is used for seeding. Dirt can indicate new ground and new opportunities for the dreamer. If the dirt is hard and dry, it reflects a drought and that means famine. The location is important; dirt on highways could mean building, landscaping, or some other endeavor. Wet dirt is mud this could signify slander, expose's, and scandals.*

19. *Computer: In prophetic contexts, it speaks to modern technology. For symbolic purposes, the computer represents the same spirit of arrogance as the Titanic represented to its creators because it is elevated to the station of deity and seeks to replace with artificial intelligence.*

20. *Cup: vessel of the vine; a spiritual symbol of oblation and outpouring. Can also symbolize an experience or a call to purpose, assignment, or charge delivered from the spirit realm to our natural one. Usually seen in dreams.*

21. *Day Break: symbolic ally, this term refers to the interruption of darkness, specifically a dark hour of trouble or sorrow with the illuminations of God.*

22. *Day of the Lord: is apocalyptic; it speaks to the times in history when God injects His wrath, His will, or a scheduled event that is ordained. These words are also prophetic, in visions and dreams the day is seen as violent cosmic wars, catastrophic weather, or earthly calamities such as plagues, famine, pestilence, or drought. (Is. 2:12, 13:6-9; Jeremiah 46:10; 1Thess. 5:2)*

23. *Degrees of Anointing: A term used to describe the varied measures of anointing different prophets receive. This meaning is important for prophets to understand in order to respect the gradual phases and stages in which their anointing appears and increases. It applies to them and to those whom they minister to. (Rom 12:3, 6; John 3:36; 1Cor: 12: 1, 4, and 9)*

24. *Desert: The deserts in prophetic experiences indicate a lonely, rejected, and barren place or land.*

25. *Divine Messenger: One who brings or gives communication from God. An angel, prophet, minister, or saint.*

26. *Divine Object Lessons: an important term that explains the living situations the Lord uses to train His messengers in the classrooms of the world. Prophets mostly are recipients of this type of training and grooming from the Lord.*

27. *Door: a symbol of lateral transition, entrance, and access to another sphere or opportunity.*

28. *Double Doors: a sign of entrance into high-powered positions or the presence of royalty, authority, and ruler ship. Also represent the entry way to palaces and to kingdoms. Indicates a welcome invitation or elevation.*

29. *Dragon: a leviathan-like (reptilian) creature; a massive version of the serpent. The dragon is Satan of old according to Revelation 12 and a constant occult symbol.*

30. *Dream Angel: an angelic being sent by God to communicate a message. In the Bible, this is a vehicle that is used in dreams and visions. Gabriel would have been one of those according to scripture. Daniel, Zechariah, Isaiah, and even Joseph all had encounters with angelic beings in their dream or vision state.*

31. Dream Language: Sleep communication or sleep talk that relies on imagery, symbolism, and signs meaningful to the dreamer to convey its message. Not all dreams are prophetic some arise as a result of inner turmoil, emotions, desire, or determination.

32. Dream Settings: This phrase explains the prophetic importance of recognizing the era, furnishings, location, and back drop of dreams.

33. Dream Scenarios: Are supernatural productions of the spirit realm of God's creation. They may be presented by dream angels, the Lord Himself, by the Holy Spirit, or the devil and his demons. The stories and situations themselves portray to the sleeper spiritual messages or reveal prophetic events on the calendar of creation.

34. Dream Thoughts: The greatest Biblical example of this is Nebuchadnezzar's prelude to his golden image dream.

35. Dreamer of Dreams: from Deuteronomy 13:1, 3, 5, a spiritual gifting where the majority of the individual's supernatural experience comes through dreams. Joseph was a prophet but his main way of prophetic reception was through dreams. His ability distinguished itself and demonstrated its prophetic link by Joseph being able to interpret his dreams and the dreams of others.

36. Dress: Article of clothing; garments worn that serve as coverings to indicate an officer's insignia and ministry representation.

37. Eight: The number of new beginnings, such as the new week in Genesis 2:2-7; this passage explains it as the number following the last day of the Lord's week. The Lord created Adam on the eighth day.

38. Emerald, and emerald green: (A) A green gemstone that prophetically symbolizes royalty and/or eternity and spoke of prosperity in nearly every area of human existence. (Ex. 28: 1-18, Ezekiel 28:13; Revelation 21:19) (B) A color from the stone after its name. It symbolizes Christian faith and the Godhead. It also speaks of divine revelation.

39. Entertainment: To hold (by entering within) to maintain influence or control over one's mind. To engage by diverting the attention from seriousness or business to pleasure.

40. Face: An appearance of the frontal view of something. An expression or confrontation. Can also mean meeting. Nodding indicates a release, revealed reaction, an approval or disapproval, or other emotion.

The fivefold ministry offices in full function:

Joel 2:28,29 and Acts 2:17, says And it shall come to pass afterward that I will pour out my spirit on all flesh, your sons and your daughters shall prophesy, your old men shall dream dreams, your young men shall see visions. {29} and also on my men servants, and on my maid servants I will pour out my spirit in those days.

The body of Christ, needs a later rain anointing, an outpour of the Holy Spirit on us. As we know, Jesus is soon to come back for a church without spot or blemish. God is still trying to position his bride {the Church} this is because the fivefold Ministry has not been restored to the fullness of what God has called it to do.

GODS ORDER FOR GROWING HIS CHURCH
Five Fold ministry in Motion~

~What is spiritual growth? What is God's view and language? Are we as God's chosen people understanding what God is really saying to the church. Do we really have spiritual ears to hear what the spirit of the Lord is saying to his bride? The body of Christ has a way of believing that they got their God all in one barrel. Most say they are spiritual enough to hear, but when I look at Revelation Chapter 2-3, what I see is even though the churches had some good qualities there was some things that the Lord had against them.

As the body of Christ come closer and learn more of who our God is it seems as if they really don't know him at all. In fact he is not a religious or a denominational God. If you ever study any other religion it boxes in the God by religion, legalism, or some type of Bondage. When we come in to serve Christ we are babes and we are lacking understanding of who we are and who we are serving. But as we mature in Chronos, (time either long or short) we should be also growing spiritually. Spiritual growth is something we must continue to do if we say we are servants of the most high it builds our relationship with the Father as well as gives us understanding of who he is. One of the prime goals of Gods church should be spiritual multiplication, this is to train up mature believers who can reproduce themselves to the third and fourth generation.

GODS ORDER FOR CHURCH GROWTH

Five- fold ministry in divine operation ~Ephesians 4:11-14

Many years ago as I had prepared for a Sunday morning sermon, as it was my Sunday to preach. I had a vision of two muscular big powerful hands coming together locking tightly with lightning and great sound. And the Holy Spirit said unto me. My five~ fold government offices must come to divine order. At that time I did not quite understand the divine revelation the Lord was streaming unto me. I continued to seek after God about what he told me and all he said at that time was, as you see the hands locking tightly together this is how I am orchestrating my body to be.

I believe in this dispensation of time we must understand our Father in heaven and ask him what it is father that you are saying to the church. The Body of Christ is sick, not only with the rampant blatant sin or delusional mindset but, we have lost our vision for what the Father has mandated us his bride to become. The Body is sick with heart failure we need a blood transfusion. Satan has lulled the body asleep with tradition, religion and legalism. Jesus was not religious, when he walked the earth for 3 and a half years what he demonstrated was teaching and preaching his kingdom and healing the sick the church was not formed unto he died. The body of Christ is stuck in the last move of God. The charismatic and the flow of the gifts, and induction of the Pastor and evangelist.

The prophets came forth in about 1980's and wasn't received or inducted to well no one looked at this office as an ordained office, when believers started talking about the Apostolic office leadership was looking crazy as if God was saying something that was not in his word. The Lord allowed me to prophesy to several Pastors about them becoming Apostles, God has been trying to change the order of how we have been taught. Think about it; in time past when the Pastor and evangelist was inducted as you see in Ephesians 4:11, Evangelist and pastors were at the end of the list in these offices most times God works from the end to the beginning of a thing. But most churches put the evangelist and pastor's office before Apostle and Prophet mainly because of how they were inducted in to the body. We still have churches that don't believe that a prophet should or can be an ordained office. (Ephesians 4:11) Amplified Bible (AMP) 11 and His gifts were [varied; He Himself appointed and gave men to us] some to be apostles (special messengers), some prophets (inspired preachers and expounders), some evangelists (preachers of the Gospel, traveling missionaries), some pastors (shepherds of His flock) and teachers.

I remember in my time of ordination, I was in a denominational church at the time, which did not even believe in prophets my Pastor at the time; was very prophetic and he heard from the lord even though he didn't fully understand the prophetic. The Lord told him that I was an office prophet and not an evangelist and he was to ordain me as so. Well I need to tell you that I was the only prophet in that region that had been ordained as a prophet. So you can understand the persecution his church, him and I endured. So many, due to ignorance fought and went against what the lord was trying to show the church. They missed it.

The Father is raising up a nation of believers who will hear what the Father is saying to the church. These will be for runners, trail blazers and pioneers, those that will pave the way, and prepare the people of God, almost like a John the Baptist mandate. People will look at them like they are crazy, misunderstand them and go against them. But God will be a driving force in them to go forward and plow through this demonic distraction that has come against the church.

God also gave me a dream, about 15 years ago stating that he is raising up an influx of leaders, officers, Ambassadors for his kingdom. In this influx, it will be Apostles, Prophets, and Pastors. But some will be in Pastors, some will run before their time, and some will misunderstand what I have called them to do. God said you will see it, He also said these that I will raise up will go through the fire, through the flood and will remain. The test will be hard because these shall endure, because of the last influx of Pastors, evangelist, prophets have miss used my grace and anointing. But I am God I will not take my anointing from them. (The gifts and office operate without repentance) Romans 11:29 (AMP) For God's gifts and His call are irrevocable. [He never withdraws them when once they are given, and He does not change His mind about those to whom He gives His grace or to whom He sends His call.

I didn't understand fully what the father was saying to me in this revelation.
As I became a Chief ~Prophet, and then a Pastor to a church I now understand more and more of what the father was saying to me. First to deal with the five-fold governmental ministries in order. Apostle and prophet receive their revelation and insight directly from God similar to the Old Testament prophets like Moses, and the New Testament Apostles received to deliver their fresh manna to the world. Apostles and Prophets are inducted into the body first hand as Gods kingdom citizens they receive revelation directly and dramatically as his first ranking agents.

In addition; Apostles and Prophets, because of their close interaction with the risen Christ, envision new converts and the church all together radically different than the other officers. Both of these officers recognize the ecclesia's call to mirror the lord's eternal kingdom. Their approach to ministry pursues a reflection of the kingdom of God and Christ.

Apostles and Prophets work together in building a new foundation for God's church. Edifying and birthing and bringing Sons and daughters to the knowledge of his truth. And equipping the body to maturity. Our main enemy is ignorance which is sin; daily believers never come to places of maturation because of the sin of ignorance. We all must hold an account for judgment someday. Whether the bema seat, or the white throne judgment. What will ours be, will it be wood, hay or straw, and when thrown in the fire being burnt up. 1 Corinthians 3:11-13 (AMP) For no other foundation can anyone lay than that which is [already] laid, which is Jesus Christ (the Messiah, the Anointed One)12 But if anyone builds upon the Foundation, whether it be with gold, silver, precious stones, wood, hay, straw, 13 The work of each [one] will become [plainly, openly] known (shown for what it is); for the day [of Christ] will disclose and declare it, because it will be revealed with fire, and the fire will test and critically appraise the character and worth of the work each person has done.

We all will have to hold an account. Apostles and Prophets seek to illuminate the hidden things of God and dispense its logic in a way to the church. The ecclesia's chief purpose is to illuminate the darkened, delusional human mind with its creator's wisdom and ideally reconnect the unsaved to their eternal God, as children of light rather than offspring of the supernatural darkness they purse after. Their mandate is to sanctify a body for him, he prepared for his eternity
Apostles and prophets are keenly skilled to deliver God's church the single power that is able to save their souls. Their job descriptions are not just to give you a house or a car, or money and opportunity. This is not the reason they operate in prophecy, signs and wonders. But it is to sanctify your soul holy first so you can understand who you are and who's you are, if you are drunken by material gain you will never be able to understand why the kingdom is on Jesus shoulders. But they have a mandate for the kingdom to receive the whole inheritance, not just a pinch.

A five-fold officer: Anyone filling one of the five- fold governmental positions of Ephesians 4:11; (apostle, prophet, evangelist, pastor and teacher).

Five: the number five is an operative number. It belongs to the virtue of grace manifested and operated as the hand of God in a life / or ministry. Anything the Lord provides freely, and it can't be paid by earthly currency, it is a gift of Grace. The number equates to hand symbolism and represents the performance of a service vow to the Lord. It particularly applies to a sacrificial service. Five also speaks the vow of devotion expressed as the power in the hands of someone to fulfill it. Hand symbolism goes way back and is brought forward by Apostle Paul in his presentation to the five-fold offices of the New Testament church. The Old Testament temple looked forward to the hands fulfillment in the New Testament church. It had five pillars to support the structure. Thus the ministries of elders and leaders are foreshadowed there.

Office/ Officer: A position of trust where agency and representative powers are granted for one's service to another. One charged with special duties and responsibility of a command conferred by a governmental authority for a public service.

Ephesians 4:11 lists the governmental ministries of the Body of Christ. These offices oversee and develop the Body of Christ. Eph. 4:12 tells us that these five governmental ministries prepare the saints for their various ministries but don't do all the ministering for the saints.

Apostle **Prophet** **Evangelist** **Pastor** **Teacher**	**Identify/acknowledge** **Re-systematize/conform** **Restore/Renew** **Prepare/equip** **Educate/ and place**	➤ ➤ **THE** ➤ **PEOPLE** ➤ **OF** ➤ **GOD**	**The Work of Ministry** ← Unto← ←←← **The Up building** **Of the Body of Christ**

These Governmental ministries are given to the church to identify, acknowledge, re-systematize and conform, restore, prepare, and educate to place the members of the Body of Christ, so that the Body can function properly. Both governmental and congregational ministries have a divine work of importance in the Body. There is also a distinct difference between the two that cannot be ignored.

Governmental Ministries Defined

Apostle: A special commissioned messenger of the Lord Jesus Christ Apostles are granted by God status and powers and delegated spherical principalities over which they rule. Apostles serve as Christ's stratospheric warriors and ambassadors in the Earth. The name for the twelve Disciples of Christ elevated to the office of Apostleship by Him during His earthly ministry. Apostles are sent ones. They are the high callers that challenge people constantly to grow up, stretch themselves, and rise above the mundane to serve God on His level. They are builders, creative, innovative, and forward driven. The Apostle promotes divine order, God's worship, and his people's priestly service to their King. They are eternity minded and want to exercise and operate Christ's eternity in the now every day. As great governors, they take leadership beyond the routine management of the church to the government of the Kingdom.

Apostolic leaders are intelligent, structured, and informative. Learning and teaching are important to them to transform people from who they were at the cross to what God made them to become forever. Their intimate relationship with the resurrected Christ makes them persuaded leaders, fervent workers, and passionate deliverers of God's truth. They potently demonstrate the powers of the age to come.

Apostolic House: The Local church institution that serves the totality of the New Testament dispensation represented by the full complement of the Ephesians 4:11 offices. The churches at Jerusalem and Corinth are strong biblical examples of the apostolic house.

Prophet: A divine functionary who serves as a spokesperson for a deity (male gender).

Prophetess: A female gender of a prophet.
Prophetesses date back as far as the Old Testament and were ascribed all the powers, authority, and competence of their counterparts. Biblical names: Miriam, Deborah, Hulda, Anna, and Phillip's daughters were God's prophetesses. Both Miriam (Exodus 15:20) and Deborah doubled as secular rulers as well. Deborah (bee) was a prophetess, judge, and the wife of Lapidoth a military leader (Judges 4:4).

Prophetic Mentorship: An essential term for the prophet's sphere of training and preparation. It explains the novice prophet who voluntarily submits to a Chief Prophet or an Apostle for the purposes of training, cultivation, and eventually God's use. Elisha and Elijah are biblical examples of this vital prophetic custom.

Prophetic Work Spectrum: it is one thing to assume the office of the prophet or to answer God's call to it. It is another to know what that office entails and the spectrum of activities and duties that accompany it. The prophetic, like any other official duty of God's Kingdom, has a basic complement of duties all prophets are to perform when called upon. The importance of knowing the work tasks of the prophet is training. Prophetic training that fully meets the demands of the office must go beyond merely teaching people to hear God and to prophesy. If the prophets' responsibility of enforcing the words they speak on the forces of darkness and compelling their manifestation into this realm is to be fulfilled, then up and coming messengers should be familiar with the full scope of their assignments and understand their corresponding skills and abilities.

Prophetic Duties: The tasks, responsibilities, and details assigned to and carried out by prophets. These include delivering the word of the Lord, inducting leadership into God's service, instituting and enacting divine government, discipline and correction, vocational declaration, counseling, and instruction. Refer to Ezra 5:1; Zech. 3; Neh. 6:14; Amos 3:7-9; Daniel 1:20; Jer. 1:5, 10 and Micah 3:8.

Evangelist: male or female gender, a member of the five-fold office that completes the line of itinerant ministers. It is the third officer of Ephesians 4:11. One of the Four Evangelists, the authors of the canonical Christian Gospels in the New Testament. A Christian participant in evangelism, such as a minister who serves as an itinerant or special preacher or a layperson who explains his or her beliefs to a non-Christian. In Christian tradition, the Four Evangelists are Matthew, Mark, Luke, and John, the authors attributed with the creation of the four Gospel accounts in the New Testament that bear the following titles: the gospels according to Matthew, Mark, Luke and John. The gospels of Matthew, Mark, and Luke are known as the Synoptic Gospels, because they include many of the same stories, often in the same sequence. Convention has traditionally held the authors to have been two of the Twelve Apostles of Jesus, John and Matthew, and two "apostolic men,"[citation needed] Mark and Luke: Matthew – a former tax collector who was called by Jesus to be one of the Twelve Apostles, Evangelism is the preaching of the Christian Gospel or the practice of relaying information about a particular set of beliefs to others with the object of conversion.

[1] The term is not restricted to any particular Christian tradition and should not be confused with Evangelicalism, a common term for a wide range of "Evangelical" Protestant churches and groups. Christians who specialize in evangelism are often known as evangelists, whether they are in their home communities or living as missionaries in the field, although some Christian traditions refer to such people as missionaries in either case. Some Christian traditions consider evangelists to be in a leadership position. They may be found preaching to large meetings or in governance roles. Christian groups who actively encourage evangelism are sometimes known as evangelistic or evangelist. The scriptures do not use the word 'evangelism', but 'evangelist' is used in (the translations of) Acts 21:8, Ephesians 4:11, and 2 Timothy 4:5.

Pastor: one who shepherds a flock of sheep; symbolically, the church of the Lord Jesus Christ. As far as the Old Testament goes, the word Pastor appears prominently as those who tend the flock of God only in the prophecies of Jeremiah and Ezekiel. The majority of those cases have the prophets rebuking Israel's shepherds for their mistreatment of God's people. In other times of pastoral mentions prophesy the coming of Christ as the true shepherd of the flock. Jeremiah in 17:16 describes himself as a pastor, although he is clearly called to be a prophet (see shepherding prophet).

The word used for pastor in the Greek is poimen. Its meaning is so expansive one wonders how the church ended up with its narrow view of the pastor's work. In a strictly natural since, from which the spiritual application of the term came from, poimen defined is a herdsman who shepherds. The pastor in this vein is one who cares for and controls the flock entrusted to him. The pastor manages, governs, and nourishes the flock with the precepts, doctrine, and dispensations of Jesus Christ. Spiritually, the Lord's invisible creation sees his pastors as priestly kings and or princes over spherical regions in which the church resides before the Lord God. Typical pastoral tasks include: watching out for enemies attempting to stalk, invade, and endanger the flock.
They are to defend the sheep from predators and threats from nature and creatures. Pastors heal Christ's wounded sheep, tend to and nurse back to health the sick ones, and seek and restore the kidnapped or wandering ones. Pastors are to love the flock.

Roeh Prophet: The Prophet whose mantle has a strong shepherding element attached to the ministry whereby responsibility for subordinate and novice prophets exists.
Pastor/Prophet Collaborative: this speaks of the prophet assigned to the local church. The distinctive of this the prophet being the higher officer according to 1 Cor 12:28-29 and Eph 4:11; in routine prophetic environments, this distinctive could be insignificant because of the setting of the local church it could create difficulty unless the prophet understands the place of the ministry in the church. In this, the prophet voluntarily submits his or her mantle under the Pastor for the duration of the assignment, much like the Lord Jesus did in coming to Earth as the divine human agent of the God-head. The Bible says that He emptied himself or He set aside His divine privileges or Godhood. (See Philipians2:7). The pastor on the other hand interacts with the prophet as more of a contractual agent, if the officer is sent by God or if the prophet grew up under the pastor. The ideal arrangement is based on the pastor's vision and calling and the prophet's ability to support and advance it. The prophet's authority is exercised as a complement to the pastors not as usurpation. If the rule in the congregation is to set the order of a pastor and not an apostle, then the prophet must see himself or herself as a staff officer. Information in this chapter on evangelist and pastor are quotations off line.

Chapter 3

The Birthing of a Prophet:

The Awakening of the Prophetic Office

~ What is a prophet?
~ What is the mantle of the Prophet?

Definitions: *(All definitions were taken from a prophetic dictionary)*

Prophet: *A divine functionary who serves as a spokesperson for a deity (male gender).*

Prophetess: *A female gender of a prophet.*
Prophetesses date back as far as the Old Testament and were ascribed all the powers, authority, and competence of their counterparts. Biblical names: Miriam, Deborah, Hulda, Anna, and Phillip's daughters were God's prophetesses. Both Miriam (Exodus 15:20) and Deborah doubled as secular rulers as well. Deborah (bee) was a prophetess, judge, and wife of Lapidoth a military leader (Judges 4:4).

Seer: *one who sees in the spirit realm and prophesies what is seen.*
Samuel judged Israel and was called a seer early in his ministry. A Seers gestures can mimic other spiritual activities that somewhat mirror and official prophet. Seers' manifestations may also be observed in strong intercessors.

Seeing Prophets: *An oversight prophet who receives his or her communication from God mostly through visions and dreams. A seeing prophet's mantle has strong Shepard ship, and Pastoral elements attached.*

Prophets Mantle: *As distinguished from the prophecy anointing this term refers to the peculiar spiritual covering that designates and empowers the prophet. The mantle serves to provoke the prophet's spirit within the officer. An official garment is discerned by other honored people and collaborated by the angelic host. The prophet's mantle is how the prophet attracts and accurately presents the word of the Lord and supports the prophet's ministry with authority. The prophet's mantle as seen in (1 Samuel*

28:14) is not only eternal and spiritual but it is the prophet's covering and contains the messenger's ministry attributes as well. See also (2 Kings 2:13, 14).

Mantle: *A loose fitting garment worn by prophets and other officials in authority to signify their position and power. The prophet's mantle reflects latitude, stature, prestige and provision for the wearer, as the license and key to act. The ward and mantle of the prophet is powerful.*

Mantle Treatment: *What is learned, practiced, and provided for the mantle to be equipped and empowered for service to the Lord.*

The above definition is beyond normal church attendance and bible studies. It is during mentorship and school of ministry, along with the Holy Spirit taking the individual on a spiritual teaching journey. (This is especially true for the Prophet and Apostle). Ministry apprenticeship is also needed for effective treating of one's mantle.

Mandate: *An official trust or authority handed over by a superior to a subordinate to give authority to act, judge, or govern as a representative of a court, country, or sovereign. This applies to jurisdictions, territories, and the execution of official businesses.*

In this chapter, you will see and learn how God takes a prophet through training and how a real prophet should operate. Further you'll understand how imperative it is for the prophet to be trained properly in order for him / her to utilize the office/gift effectively. There are forty two functions that God has anointed the office to do. Therefore, please do not be misled that training is not essential. Just as we as ministers of the gospel must study the word of God to show ourselves approved, we must also be trained in our gifts or office. Whether God blesses you with a prophetic mentor or not, you need to seek God for proper training.

In 1 Kings 19:19~ God used Elijah to mentor/father Elisha. When the training was done, because of what he had experienced, Elisha asked for more. If Elisha had stayed doing his own family business, he would have never been as effective as he became as a result of what he learned. He received a mantle to seal the completion of his teaching. As a result, he was able to do mightier exploits than his mentor. In order to qualify for a higher level you must obtain prophetic competence.

Prophetic Competence: *The status and condition of a prophet's skill in relation to the task(s) and requirements of the office.*

This definition includes the prophet's conflict with the spiritual & carnal resistance to the word of the Lord from his/ her ability to overcome the resistance. See Elisha's earlier days in 2 Kings. This is not about your gift and anointing, but submitting yourself to the time to be trained and valuing your prophetic gift/office enough to allow proper training and development so that you'll be able to operate on point whenever God needs to use you.

Well trained prophets will weigh their words. Therefore, wisdom is needed, being wise as a serpent and harmless as a dove, (Matt: 10:16, Behold, I am sending you out like sheep in the midst of wolves; be wary and wise as serpents, and be innocent {harmless, guileless, and without falsity} as doves.) There is no need to prove the office or gift. If you try to do so, you'll fail every time. It is also important not to allow anyone else to push you to a place just because they want to see a show.

Sometimes we say things just because it comes to our mind. As such, this is why a prophet/prophetic people must be driven by wisdom; if not we can make a shipwreck and damage or even kill another life. Please note: it is not about how well you can prophesy or give a deep revelation, but it is about getting proper balance, development, and training to work what God has given you. Also keep in mind that every word before it is weighed and discerned can go one way or the other. There are two powers connected to our words: the power of light and the power of darkness. Remember the scripture (Proverbs 18:21-death and life are in the power of the tongue, and they who indulge in it shall eat the fruit of it [for death or life].) So don't add to the warfare.

When the Lord has divinely given you information for someone, most of the time warfare will come and you will feel what I call the warfare fears, confusion, or you will wrestle with, 'Is this God or is it me?' However, to alleviate some of the drama we put ourselves through, first, we must make sure the word wasn't for us. If it wasn't then just weigh the word. For example: who is the word for? Is it someone you don't like or who doesn't like you? Or is it someone that won't receive the word after you have properly weighed it and know it's what the Lord has charged you to deliver?

Sometimes when we know a person or have heard something about a person and the Lord gives us a word to deliver, it is not always received. In a case like that, follow the steps in the above paragraph. This is a classic example of why a prophet/prophetic people cannot be in everything or in everyone's business. If you expect to hear clearly from God and to flow effectively, you cannot be tainted with information.

The Reputation of a Prophet/Prophetic People

As a prophet/prophetic people, your reputation is being formed in the first 3 to 5 years of your prophetic walk or gift. God is building a prophetic resume for you. Humility and obedience is a prerequisite to being a properly trained prophet. While in the development stage, you can't afford to ignore or allow weeds and bad seeds or attitude problems to affect you. If you do, you will not be a useable vessel. This is why often we see prophetic people or prophets that are gifted but will be off in *their delivery. This happens when they have not been fully healed or delivered. Remember that the gift/office comes without repentance, so a person can operate out of their gift or office and still have a reputation that stinks. This would be a classic example of a bad prophetic resume. Also, you must understand that when things come up against you, check yourself first. This may be God's way of stripping you of some things like pride, haughtiness, or disobedience. However painful, allow the Holy Spirit to rid you of these areas. If not, they will hinder your prophetic walk.*

A Pastor's Acceptance of an Established Prophet

First and foremost, you must know that all Pastors/leaders want to obey the voice of God, unless they have no God in them. Your overseers may seem as if they are not in agreement with you. They actually have the right to be concerned. As the Pastor(s), they dare not allow anybody to come in their church and do anything seemingly ungodly (this is how some see it). Prior to allowing you to operate, it is important that a leader knows your spirit, has a relationship with you, and knows that you are a reliable member in order for him or her to allow you to take charge in his or her edifice.

As believers we have a tendency to blame others for what we're doing wrong. Some of us even look and expect to receive stuff from leaders that God intended for us to obtain on our own. Although called and gifted, some of us have no integrity and are not responsible enough to handle what we possess. Therefore, we must understand that God has given us Bishops and Pastors to watch over our souls. You must trust that they will know when it is time to release you to operate, because sometimes when you think you're ready you are not.

Please note, a Pastor will not allow anyone that has not proven themselves to stand before his/her church and wound the sheep that they Sheppard. Although appointed by God, you must demonstrate consistency and Prophetic Competence. There are so many people in the body of Christ that have a history of church hopping. This is a spirit of rebellion. If the leader does not do and hear what they say, they leave the church. We must understand when this happens, it becomes difficult for a leader to trust or determine who you really are, what is working in you, and if you will have longevity.

On the other hand, there are some Pastors who really don't know how to engage the prophet or even know where to place them in the church. While there are still some Pastors who don't even know how to recognize a prophet, one thing you must do if you know you are an office prophet is submit your prophetic rank to your leaders and submit yourselves to much prayer. This continual prayer is not for them. The prayer is for all you can and will see prophetically as well as what the spirit of the Lord is saying to you about you. Don't be discouraged if you don't see results right away, just keep praying.

When you are in a church as a member, you are under the auspices of your Bishop/Pastor. You are not ranked above them. If you submit to God first and then to the headship God has put over that house, all will come together. In doing so, it will keep down a lot of the mess/confusion of the other sheep. Submit to authority when needed. Don't play on the power you may possess. Don't down play others' servant hood as this could create "prophetic seduction." (This is a prophet using his/her mantle to influence others into their own desires for personal gain and private advantage.) Prophets should not pull on the sheep to talk against the Pastors. You must keep your spirit untainted. If not, you will be a dangerous vessel bringing division instead of unity.

Jeremiah 1:4, 5, 6-12

(4) Then the word of the Lord came to me saying (5) before I formed thee in the belly I knew thee, and before thou comest forth out of the womb I sanctified thee and I ordained thee a prophet unto the nations.(6) Then said I Ah, Lord God! Behold I cannot speak for I am a child.(7) But the Lord said unto me, Say not I am a child for thou shalt go to all that I shall send thee and what so ever I command thee thou shalt speak. (8) Be not afraid of their faces, for I am with thee to deliver thee saith the Lord.(9) Then the Lord put forth his hand and touched my mouth and the Lord said unto me behold I have put my words in thy mouth. (10) See I have this day set thee over the nations and over the kingdom; to root out and to pull down and to destroy, and to throw down, to build and to plant. (11) Moreover the word of the Lord came unto me saying Jeremiah what seest thou? In addition, I said a rod of an almond tree (12) then said the Lord unto me Thou hast seen well for I will hasten my word to perform it.

What equips the prophet? Before the Lord releases the Prophetic Officer in his/her office, He puts the prophet through an intensive training program like boot camp. I call this the prophetic training through the Holy Ghost. God's way of equipping for ministry is mainly spiritual. The prophet's function is largely supernatural, although people think it's nothing more than getting ready for the Lord's service, hearing, and speaking what saith the Lord. For many people, prophetic preparation starts with God isolating beginners and streaming prophetic dreams and visions to them. Nonetheless, dreams and visions is how God presents Himself to the novice (new prophet). The reason visions and dreams are the starting point of prophetic education is because God introduces Himself and awakens the prophet's revelatory faculties through them.

Once the novice prophet is made aware of the calling, the Lord's preparatory methods shift to more intense and demanding activities. You'll find that God will diligently go after the inherent and nurtured pride, arrogance, and independence of the young prophet since submission is the requirement of prophetic service. Once this begins, things really get interesting.

Some of us have seemed to have something peculiar about us all of our lives. That is because you are a chosen child of God. We all have testimonies or experiences in our lives with the Lord. However being a prophet is deeper than that. Although in church you may hear people say "for all you deep people" or *"you are too deep for me", the Holy Spirit shared with me that it's not about appearing to be deep. One must go deep in order to find the things of God. We must understand that in order for us to reach or operate in our prophetic office, God has got to stir us up. This stirring may start to rise up within your local church setting where God may begin to reveal things to you. You may begin to give prophetic utterances, speaking the word of God or perhaps receiving an increase in discernment to the point where you are seeing the sin in the church and you have been released to flow in all the revelational gifts. As this intensifies, so will the dreams/ visions and various other areas. Thus, the prophetic ministry begins to manifest in your life.*

Although others may begin to see and acknowledge your prophetic office, for a season prophesying may be the last thing God wants of His new student. His primary focus is resetting the new prophet's attitude, perspectives, and priorities to perform reliable prophetic services. In God's initial training of a prophet, the lessons are experiential. The curriculum seems multidimensional and the tests excruciating. However, He is really trying to get His prophet ready for service. The prerequisites of learning are: spirituality, morality, integrity, discipline, and obedience. God will raise up trainers and mentors that he selects to help the novice prophet through the process.

The developing prophet will encounter and interact with every sphere of human existence so that the mantle is equipped to treat its every condition. This is just the first stage in your prophetic journey. While in this stage, you may seem to be functioning as a prophet, but you are not yet appointed to the prophetic office. This means that you do not have the authority to stand in the Office of the Prophet. It also means that you have not been permanently appointed to that position, you are walking it out first. During this period, you will rise up prophetically in the local church. Also during this period, you won't even know that God has appointed you to the office or geared you for it. Often, the church will not even recognize that God has set you apart for that office. This stage is the covering of the prophet's appointment. Very often, the prophets of God will rise up as insignificant individuals in the local body and most times they won't fit in with the local church or congregants.

The prophet, in the spirit, is like the story of the bad seed (child) which turns into the good child or the Ugly Duckling who becomes the beautiful swan. They don't fit in at first. No one seems to like them because their mouth is too big and/ or they are too holy. Everybody stays away from or is afraid of them because of what they see or perceive. The prophet is not part of the crowd. Most prophets are looked at as not normal. Whether this is experienced in the adolescent or adult stage of their life, very often the prophet feels out of place and is always asking what is wrong with me.

Although dismayed at times, there is always something inside the prophet that drives them to press. Most times, a prophet will pull out of a crowd or avoid them altogether. Some are natural introverts or like being alone. The novice prophet really thinks that others don't like them. It would appear as if the novice prophet will go through an emotional roller coaster as he/she is going through the process of their intense training in becoming the prophet God has appointed them to be. When God gets through with you as a prophet, you are going to be able to go anywhere, any place, any country and to any denomination. No matter where you go, you'll carry the same authority because you have been appointed as an officer to the universal church.

Prophets deal with many obstacles in their training. In this section, we'll discuss the process Jeremiah the prophet went through.

What Jeremiah had to face: *There were two types of fears Jeremiah had to overcome: (1) the fear of loss and (2) the fear of rejection. God calls us to replace our fears of loss with faith in provision. Our own fear becomes our bondage. We must release and surrender in order to produce security and rest. Total surrender requires trust in him.*

Surrender to fear of loss:

Possessions:
- *(Mark 8:36 amp.) "For what does it profit a man to gain the whole world and forfeit his life?"*

Reputation:
- *(Mark 8:37 amp.) "For what can a man give as an exchange, compensation, or ransom in return for his blessed life in the eternal kingdom of God?"*

Selfishness:
- *(Mark 8:34, 35 amp.) "And Jesus called (to him) the throng with his disciples and said to them, If anyone intends to come after me, let him deny himself {forget, ignore, disown and lose sight of himself and his own interest} and take up his cross and {joining me as a disciple and siding with my party} follow with me continually cleaving steadfastly to me."*

Needs:
- *(Matt 6:32-34 amp.) "For the gentiles {heathen} wish for and crave and diligently seek all these things and your heavenly father knows well that you need them all. But seek {aim at and strive after} first, of his entire kingdom and his righteousness {his way of doing and being right} and then all these things taken together will be given you. So do not worry or be anxious about tomorrow, for tomorrow will have worries and anxieties of its own; sufficient for each day is its own trouble."*

Relationship and life:

- *(Matt 10:37-39 amp.) "He who loves {takes pleasure in} father or mother than in me is not worthy of me; and he who loves {and takes more pleasure in} son or daughter more than in me is not worthy of me. And he who does not take up his cross and follow me {cleave steadfastly to me} conforming wholly to my examples in living, and if need be in dying also is not worthy of me. Whoever finds his {lower} life will lose it {the higher life} and whoever loses {lower} life on my account will find it {higher life}."*

Surrender to the fear of rejection:

- *The message that Jeremiah carried was not popular.*
- *Jeremiah had to face rejection and loss because of the message he carried. He was called to speak against the moral depravity of the culture he lived in. There were seven kings that reigned during his ministry. Three kings that reigned were: Manasseh, Jehoiakim and Zedekiah. (Note: this nation had forsaken God because of the leader's sins.) They were worshipping Idols, and Baal Asher, which were immoral and wicked. Therefore, they were morally and spiritually deprived.*

He was rejected by his family:

- *(Jeremiah 12:6) "For even your brothers and the household of your father, even they have dealt treacherously with you, even they have cried aloud after you. Do not believe them, although they might say nice things."*

He was rejected by his friends:

- *(Jeremiah 20:10) "For I have heard the whispering of many, terror on every side! Denounce him yes, let us denounce him! All my trusted friends watching for my fall."*

He also never married:

- *(Jeremiah 16:1) read verses 1 through 13 "the word of the Lord also came to me saying, you shall not take a wife for yourself nor have sons and daughters in this place."*

Although we in the body of Christ must deal with issues of rejection to some degree, it is sometimes the hardest thing to be rejected and yet maintain love for the very ones who rejected us. Thank God for Jesus, our greatest example. It is vitally important that prophets get the understanding of why they must embrace rejection as if it was given to them as a gift. In this, they must be able to operate and function properly in the midst of haters and those who reject them and still remain balanced spiritually to give a word from God with demonstration and power, not out of mere flesh. Take heart in knowing you are bearing this cross for Christ.

Deliverance from Rejection:

- *As we look through the book of Jeremiah we find several important means by which healing and the courage to go forth came to him. Although known as the weeping and insecure prophet, he still was obedient to what the Lord said to do.*

Intimacy:

- *The healing and courage Jeremiah needed came through intimacy with God. Jeremiah stayed at a posture so when fear, rejection, or hatred tried to come over him; he went into his secret place with the father (God). While in there, he told Daddy (God) all about it and this is when his healing took place. (Jeremiah 9:23-24).*

Belonging & Identity:

- *He found belonging and identity in God. God was his encourager. This is why a prophet must stay close to God, having a lifestyle of fasting, consecration, and prayer (Jeremiah 15:19).*

Destiny:

- *He found out that God called him to this, not man. In this no man could pluck him out of the hand of God. He knew his destiny was in God's hands.*

Favor:

- *He found divine favor with God because of his obedience and reliance on God alone. God would perform every word that would proceed out of his mouth (Jeremiah 1:11, 12).*

Defense:

- *He found out that God was his defender. Man can do nothing but kill your flesh, {it needs to die} but cannot kill you. God told Jeremiah He would make him a defense city. God was Jeremiah's defender. God said He would watch over His word to perform it (Jeremiah 1:7, 8) and (Jeremiah 15: 20, 21). As Jeremiah came to the end of his calling, he clearly saw how God repeatedly showed up for him as well as fulfilled every word He had spoken to him. He also demonstrated that no matter what anyone thought of him, he was going to do the will of God.*

Do we believe that the Lord can show up for us in the same way he did for the prophet Jeremiah?

- *Jeremiah had finally learned the secret throughout his entire walk- He ended up being a God pleaser instead of a man pleaser. Jeremiah, the weeping, insecure prophet had become one of God's Champion Prophets.*

CHAPTER 3 SECTION 2

HUMILITY- (A PRE-REQUISITE)

A broken vessel with love in the heart and possess maturity

Definitions: *(all definitions are from prophetic and bible dictionaries)*

Humility:
- *A state or quality of being humble*
- *Freedom from pride and arrogance*
- *A lowliness of mind*
- *A modest estimate of a sense of one's own worthiness through imperfection & sin.*

Maturity:
- *Mature*
- *Brought by natural process to completeness or growth & development*
- *Fitted by growth & development for any function, action or state; full grown, ripe fullness of growth.*

Brokenness:
- *The state or quality of being broken*
- *Unevenness, not working properly*
- *Behaving strangely*

In this Section we will learn how God takes the prophet/prophetic person through the school of charm, brokenness, and humility.

1 Corinthians 13:1-10 amp.

If I can speak in the tongues of men and (even) of angles but have not love (that reasoning, intentional, spiritual devotion such as is inspired by God's love) I am only a noisy gong or a clanging cymbal. And if I have prophetic powers (the gift of interpreting the divine will and purpose) and understand all secret truths and mysteries and possess all knowledge, and have (sufficient) faith so that I can remove mountains, but have not love(God's love in me) I am nothing (a useless nobody). Even if I give out all that I have (to the poor in providing food) and if I surrender my body to be burned, in order that I may glory, but have not love (God's love in me) I gain nothing. Love endures long and is patient and kind; love never is envious nor boils over with jealousy, is not boastful it does not display itself haughtily. It is not conceited (arrogant and inflated with pride) it is not rude (unmannerly) and does not act unbecomingly. Love (God's love in us) does not insist on its own rights or its own way. For it is not self-seeking; it is not touchy or fretful or resentful; it takes no account of evil done to it (it pays no attention to a suffered wrong). It does not rejoice at injustice and unrighteousness, but rejoices when right and truth prevail. Love bears up under anything and everything that comes, it is ever ready to believe the best of every person; its hopes are fadeless under all circumstances and it endures everything (without weakening). Love never fails (never fades out or becomes obsolete or comes to an end). As for prophecy (the gift of interpreting the divine will and purpose) it will be fulfilled and pass away (it will lose its value and be superseded by truth). Our knowledge is fragmentary (incomplete and imperfect). And our prophecy (our teaching) is fragmentary (incomplete and imperfect). But when the complete and perfect (total) comes, the incomplete and imperfect will vanish away (become antiquated, void and superseded).

We need to see that God deals with a man or a woman in terms of his or her entire lifetime as they invite Him to move towards their destiny. At times it may appear as if He's not in a hurry at all. While other times, He takes us on a crash course to learn some hard but necessary lessons. He does this in order to get us ready for the purpose He has called us to.

The School of Brokenness:
Brokenness is what rids a man of any confidence in his own soul's resources. In looking at the life of Moses, we see that forty years of secular training in the finest leadership schools that Egypt had to offer, he realized he was called to be a believer. Unbroken during this time, he then began knocking off the Egyptian army one by one. Although understanding this new found conviction, his efforts only got him banished to the desert. It was while in the desert that he became broken and at the age of 80, we know Moses as being the meekest on the Earth. Being broken made the difference in his life. One who has been through God's school of brokenness is no longer marked by obstinacy, hardness, and sharpness which are signs of an unbroken vessel.

Meekness is the true sign of brokenness. It is Jacob walking with a limp and Paul admitting he was a persecutor of the saints. Meekness is not the same as weakness; but it is characterized by a humble reliance on God's power and strength. Moses relied on the power of God, not his own power. We see Moses not defending himself to his accusers but rather falling on his face in intercession while God moves dramatically to defend him. One who is meek will also exhibit sensitivity to others. They will be approachable and teachable, instead of hard and unentreatable.

The one who is meek is not arrogantly independent; but rather, recognizes his/her need for unity. The more confidence a person has in themselves at the beginning of this kind of school, the longer and harder the breaking will be. However, when God accomplishes the work He is after, mighty signs and wonders will be demonstrated through the person because both will declare that the credit and glory belongs to God.

Some will say, 'I am humble' or 'I don't need to be humbled' or 'I am not like Moses, Paul or Jacob'. However, I beg to differ. We have so much stuff in our soul that we don't even realize what is there. We can't trust our flesh. It is deceitful and above all wicked. The Father knows all. He is the potter. He made you and He knows just what needs to be done in you and how long it will take to do it in you. When the season comes in our lives for God to take us through the course of humility, we tend to look crazy and begin asking Him questions like: 'God where am I or who am I?' and 'What is this all about God?' We even start blaming other people for what we are going through or begin rebuking the devil.

During this process, it is important that you always begin looking at yourself first and then ask God what it is He wants to do in you. Although it may seem as if the devil is after you through people, I am here to tell you it is really God. (Rom 9:21 Amp.) "Has the potter no right over the clay, to make out of the same mass (lump) one vessel for beauty and distinction and honorable use, and another for menial or ignoble and dishonorable use." (Jeremiah 18:6) "Oh house of Israel can I not do with you as this potter does says the Lord. As the clay is in the potters hand so are you in my hand, O house of Israel."

God's ways and means of introducing us to the school of brokenness can be different as well as difficult. Sometimes brokenness can appear to look like a failure or that something is wrong in a person's life. However, this accomplishes the transformation from self-confidence to God confidence. We must remember that God knows just what it will take to bring us to the end of ourselves. If you are one who has experienced exceptional brokenness, hurt or calamity in your life; you just might be one of God's projects in motion.

The School of Humility:

Humility is essential for usefulness in the Kingdom of God. It is especially essential for his prophets. We must be free from pride and haughtiness so that our ministry does not vaunt itself or attract others to us. Rather, it must represent the testimony of Jesus Christ and giving Him all glory. God says He resists the proud but gives to the humble. Therefore humility is not low self-esteem as it may appear or as some may think, but it is the absence of oneself or the freedom from a pre-occupation with self. We must come to know at the heart level and make peace with the fact that by our flesh, apart from Him, we can do nothing (and at the same time through Him we can do all things).

Someone who is humble is free from having to defend, prove, or explain his or herself. It is freedom to serve in the lowest or highest position that God decides to place them into. It is not gained by measuring ourselves to others. We sometimes have a tendency to compare ourselves to others. For example, some may say, "I don't preach like him/her, that person is so anointed" or "I can't sing like she can". Others may be the reverse and think too highly of themselves. It is vitally important that God in ourselves and in others, and see what he sees in us at his point of view.

In Is. 6:1-5, Isaiah got a glimpse of God and suddenly he had a right perspective about himself. It resulted in a confession and then a commission. He did not think more highly than he ought or poorly then he ought of himself. He had a sober and proper perspective of himself. I don't believe we have the capacity within ourselves to rightly assess apart from God. Scripture talks about love being the key to every facet of ministry. Nothing will work if we do not walk or humble ourselves in it. Therefore, if we have motive regarding why we want to operate and be used of God, then pride is at our back door and we have truly missed it. Let love be the motivation.

When the Lord began to birth forth the gifts in me, I had an Elder tell me that he had a vision of me preaching to multitudes of people and he saw my name in lights. He further went on to say that he saw me at a National level. Now before he had told me this, I didn't think I was such a great preacher. But as a result, pride began to set in and being a novice and infantile in the Lord, I allowed it to puff my head up. My motivation became what he saw and not what the Lord intended. As a result the Lord began taking me through the humbling process, which allowed me to see Him while letting me realize that it was not about me.

The result:

The goal / objective of the necessary process is to bring the prophet to the place of utter and total dependence on God. To become a doer of God's will, a vessel of honor meat for the Master's use, useful to the King's service, a sure enough friend of God and a carrier of God's own heart. The prophet is carefully chiseled to become a critical foundation stone in the church today.

CHAPTER 3 SECTION 3

The First steps in Prophecy

Preparation in prayer

In terms of preparation, prayer is absolutely vital in the prophetic. Prayer and prophecy are linked together in the communication process: both involve listening before talking. Now I must say, in order to be a prophet you must have a prayer life. A relationship with God is paramount in order to hear Him clearly. Getting into the habit of listening more instead of talking so much will also help in hearing not only when He is speaking but how to decipher His voice at every level.

Have you ever had this happen to you: you start praying for your situation and halfway through, the Holy Spirit speaks to you about someone else's situation? This is God beginning to develop the burdens of others in your spirit. Sometimes it will be an impression on your spirit or a weighty feeling and no words. Other times you will see people or things. This is why it is vital to have a prayer life. If you just pray once in a while, you will not understand the God language He is speaking to you. One thing a prophet/ or prophetic person must understand is that you have a built-in intercessor gift.

In addition to an active prayer life, we also need to have faith and believe that whatever we are praying for God to do is already done by faith. In doing so, this will increase our faith level and our ability to hear and receive the answers to our prayers. Sometimes, even prior or during prayer, we'll feel a release in our spirit right away. While other times you may not feel or see any evidence in the physical realm. During those times, you must believe that something has changed in the atmosphere and in your spirit.

The wonderful thing about prayer is that you can talk to God about anything; anytime, anywhere. It also allows you to open up your spirit and go places with and in God. We need to always keep the channel of communication open as much as possible. Equal to us praying, asking the Holy Spirit to continually speak to us is just as important {1Thess 5:16, 19 says always rejoice, constantly pray, and in everything give thanks. For this is God's will for you in Christ Jesus. Do not extinguish the spirit.}

Meditation

Next to prayer and faith, meditation is very important. Meditation has been part of the relationship with God for thousands of years. Scripture constantly mentions it, particularly in the Book of Psalms. Meditation simply means to consider deeply, to reflect, and to be absorbed in thought. It is always good to sit and meditate on the things of God, His word, and how good He is to us.

I am sure all of us can think of situations in our lives where unforeseen things have happened that set or changed the course of our lives. In pondering on those things, it is always good to meditate on how awesome God was when He brought us through. Prophets in the Old Testament were always recounting the words, prophesies, and encounters they had with God.

Waiting on God

Waiting on God is vital. It is good to have a notebook because God speaks in the most peculiar places and times. I remember the times in my earlier walk when I kept a notebook in my car. I did this because God would always speak to me during times that I never expected Him to. Sometimes, by the time I finished writing what He was saying, I would end up with two or three pages. Then, there were those times He would tell me He had to talk with me. Meaning, I had to physically and mentally get to a place of quietness so He could speak to me.

Sometimes waiting on God means letting Him know that you love Him and take pleasure in who He is. There will be times you may get nothing when waiting for Him to speak. During those times, don't be discouraged because if He doesn't speak initially, He'll always speak eventually and we need to be ready when He does. Waiting on God also means we need to come to a place of quietness and stillness. Not only should we find a quiet place, but more importantly, we should learn to still the clamoring from within our minds and hearts. If we have a lot of stuff on our minds, we cannot wait properly. Meditation (thinking deeply, absorbed in thought) and waiting upon God go hand in hand.

Meditation and waiting on God in the Christian faith is the filling of mind and heart with thoughts of God. In essence, becoming conscious. In this quiet, still activity, God drops His word like the morning dew bringing a clear refreshing to our souls and spirits.

Speaking in Tongues

Speaking in tongues, for those who have the gift, is a very important part of the devotional life and relationship with God. It edifies our spirit and renews our mind. I love to pour out of my heart to God in whatever situation I am in. Whether I am in pain or don't know what to say, I have an expectation that when I speak in tongues, somehow God is going to break in and do *something because this is the language we have between us.*

Expectation

If we are going to move in anything, whether it is faith, supernatural gifts, preaching the gospel, or whatever we are doing for God, we need to have a sense of expectation. We as believers should never live a day without expectation. For each and every day we wake up, there should be a level of expectation in our circumstances that God is going to do something for us today. Remember, we are living in a prophetic hour and church age.

I believe God wants His people to move in prophetic situations daily and we should have an expectancy that God will move. For example: If the Lord is using me to prophesy, I already believe that God is not only speaking into the situation but he is also speaking into the very life of the person that the word is for. So, with this in mind, that person should begin to have an expectancy that God is going to start manifesting what has been spoken. This is not only for the receiver, but also for the person who God is using to speak the prophetic word. Once we get a balance in understanding how God speaks to us, we can expect Him to use us. A prerequisite for Him using us is to believe He can speak through us and that we have the mind of Christ {1 Cor 2:16}.

Operation

In opening your spirit to the Lord, He will allow you to develop a burden and concern for other people. As you flow in the prophetic, these elements will become key components as God begins to lay people on your heart to pray for. How many times have we allowed people to pray or prophesy over us and not know if they even have a burden or concern for us one way or another?

Burdens reveal the very heart of God. When we have a burden or concern for something or someone we are praying for, the Holy Spirit begins forming those burdens into words. As the word begins to form, we will feel a pulling in the spirit to do or say something. This pulling will form a sense of conviction that produces expression. Once we have become convinced that God wants to say something as a result of the burden, the desire to express it will be strong. This is called the process of prophecy.

Sometimes we need to stir up the gift of prophecy. Again, this begins with keeping your spirit open to receive the burden or concern followed by knowing that if He gives you the burden, He intends to speak or act. Our position at that time should be one of expectancy for however He decides to flow. Please note: the burden God gives us for another person is not one that we have developed on our own; but as a result of our obedience and spirit being open to His will. Remember, He chose us to work with Him because it's a declaration of intent. He wants to speak and we are the chosen vessel.

In being used by God, we must have faith and possess the right spirit. We must never move on our own volition. Remember, the objective is to have blessings, healing, and/or restoration manifested in the life of the person ministered to. Therefore, when we go into places, always be prepared beforehand because you never know when God may decide to use you.

Other things to look for when releasing Gods word

The Blind Spot

A blind spot by definition is an area of our lives that we don't see. When God addresses a blind spot, sometimes we don't always get it. Sometimes we may have to meditate on it for a while or have a really good friend to break it down and tell us the truth. Have you ever had a prophetic word come to you and when the person gave the word you didn't agree with it for one reason or another? A few years ago, I had two different people give me a word from the Lord. The word was that the Lord was taking me to a level that He would not allow any man to hinder. He further said He was a jealous God. Initially, I didn't think this was from God. However, a few years later, the Lord began manifesting the word that was given to me. I'm highlighting this because there will be times where God may release you to give a word to someone and it may touch a blind spot in them. Should this happen, seek to make sure the word is from God. If so, trust the word and stand on it. We can't guard God's word nor can we worry if it was received or not. When God is addressing something in the future, you're not in it.

Being Dogmatic has no wisdom

An attitude you might want to avoid is a Dogmatic one. The definition for dogmatic is: asserting opinions in a doctrinaire or arrogant manner; opinionated. God is not a dogmatic God. He is a judge and sword. He will expose. However, if the Lord uses you as His vessel, you must not be dogmatic. We must be humble and stand flat footed when the word of God comes. Do not debate God's word. It doesn't belong to you. Again, He will guard His own word. He doesn't need your help. Example: "Well I don't care what you say; this is GOD" or "You are wrong and I am right". Putting your flesh in the situation is never a way to offer ministry to people, either they will receive or not. Your job is to just deliver the mail and let God do the rest. Sometimes you will miss it. If someone tells you that they are not receiving the word you gave, just respond graciously and with kindness. Never rebuke them. Remember, you the best to manifest Christ-like attributes in the situation. One thing you must not do is justify yourself. It is unfruitful. This is between them and God.

Don't become a personal Prophet

Watering down a prophetic word causes more problems than it solves. Every prophet will be tested in this area of his or her training. Example: Sometimes, in my earlier walk (novice), the Lord would give me a word and, because of the level of my faith at the time, I didn't give all the details of that prophetic word. Instead, I said things like: "God loves you", "He has a plan for your life", or "He wants to bless you". This is called watering down a word. When God is streaming a word to you, sometimes you must wait until you know all of what God is really saying. Never go out in the spirit before God. Say it the way God is saying it. Don't take out details. When we do this, we make the word unrecognizable to the recipient. He or she may have been praying to God about a situation and He wants to use you in the matter. By editing everything, it challenged your faith and just held the words in reverse. Don't walk in doubt. This is not about you, just flow.

Think of this, when a hungry person that is sick gets a word like this it is like giving chicken broth to a starving person. However, to the person who is healthy and has been working hard, it is not enough. He or she is looking for meat and potatoes. Watering down a word will cause you to become less effective in ministry. Be mindful, if people are in an era where they don't want to be exposed, they may want a watered down word. However, if people are looking for God to answer their cry, they don't want a message they cannot relate to. If you are not careful, wolves in sheep's clothing will come after you to seduce you and try to make you their personal prophet.

Following a flow

Another way the Lord can release a word through you is by you following the flow of the spirit. Your trust is completely in Him when you are ministering to someone. You already know in your spirit the word spoken to you is of the Lord. However uncomfortable you may feel in walking out in faith and not knowing the full word God has given, humble yourself and let the Spirit of the Lord lead, guide, and direct you in all truth. No matter what, stand on your faith and flow within your spirit man. The role of the spirit man is to support and facilitate the decisions of the spiritual man. You are not on your own. In addition to this, the flow of the word will come like the flow of living water, a continuous flow. At this level, you are being used outside of your own capacity of understanding.

Guarding against an unteachable spirit

An area you want to guard against is an unteachable spirit. Do you know some people that are' know-it-alls'? They are always right in every situation. Most times, they will never admit they're wrong. Well, this could be an unteachable spirit. Attempting to teach, counsel, and give a word to this type of person can be difficult. If you are not someone that is in their circle or a person that they respect or like, they will not receive from you. Most times, this kind of person is in rebellion and doesn't know it. As a prophet, you must guard against this kind of spirit. It has haughtiness, pride, self-centeredness, and self-righteousness in it. This is not a vessel 'meet for the Master's use'. As the prophet is being trained, the Lord will have this unseasoned prophet miss it in order to humble and show him or her what he or she needs to get rid of. Sadly, most of these people don't even recognize it. They want to still be right. As we minister the word of the Lord to others, we too must be very careful not to fall prey in this area.

CHAPTER 3 SECTION 4

A Prophetic Crawl or A Prophetic walk

- The Making of the Prophet
- Developing Character

Definition: (All definitions were taken from a prophetic dictionary and Webster's)

Character
- A person marked by notable or conscious traits
- A noticeable quality about a person or thing
- A behavior that is different than others
- To walk blameless
- To be faithful, contrite, fearing God; Holy and humble

In this section, we'll be dealing with the development of the prophet in training and why God pushes him/her to produce character.

In the book of Numbers, its interesting how Balaam, who delivered very accurate prophetic words and gave a messianic prophesy, was called a false prophet in the New Testament. Why? The answer is, he had character issues.

There are times we may experience prophets who appear to be off in their delivery and hence we declare them false. Although the Bible does speak of false prophets, we must understand that the Lord will allow a novice prophetic person or a prophet to experience those off times in an effort to sharpen and build character even while they are going forth in ministry. The bottom line is, God will deliberately allow you to miss it sometimes just so He can develop you as He designed and so that you are not operating on your own volition. Although you may have the gift, it is imperative that you learn how to crawl before you can walk. Just as it is with a baby becoming a toddler. He or she must learn how to crawl, then walk. If you don't go through this process, you will fall.

During the training of a prophet, he/she will encounter many experiences while on his or her journey. For example, the prophets may know that they are hearing from God, but can't figure out or understand the backlash or attack(s) behind delivering the word. For the prophet/prophetic person, God will take him or her through an intense training in every area of his or her walk. In an effort to perfect what He has deposited, the Lord will heavily deal with character issues in the prophet. During this time, it will seem as if everything and everyone is against you-church, leadership, family, and friends. Your personal life will appear to be under attack as well. Although it may appear or even be what you are experiencing, please know that God will allow those situations to happen in order to buffet you.

During this period, the novice prophet cannot quite understand why the devil is using the church people to tear down his or her character. But what you must understand is, it is God's way of correcting your flesh and to change your way of thinking. It will also get you to forgive when you have been hurt. As Jesus said, "forgive them for they know not what they do". This is not about the person that caused the hurt, but it is about whether you will forgive that person. If you can't, the Father cannot make you into what He wants. Most prophetic people are very opinionated. Because of this, it can become very difficult for God to use the prophet/prophetic person to deliver His word. In short, your flesh must die.

The way up is down

Humility (Phil 2: 3-7, 1 Pet 5:1-7)

It is the humble that are exalted and the proud become abased. If we attempt to lift ourselves up, we stumble. If we get low, we will be exalted by God. Letting go of stuff is the way to receive and to become humble. Give up your own right to be wrong and watch humility, lowliness, and selflessness become a priority in your life.

Surrender (Mk 8:24, 25 Mk 10: 29, 30)

If we try to save our lives (in the flesh), we will lose it. But if we let go of our lives, we will find it. We must give in order to get. We must sow in order to reap. When you're weak in Him, then you are made strong. If we can't surrender, we will lose with God.

Brokenness (2 Cor 12:9, 10)

It is when we face the terms of our inadequacies that we learn that we can confidently rely upon God's adequacy. The greatest is the servant of all. Your brokenness is to bring you low. Sometimes we can't see that our flesh is in the way until we become broken. In the broken place, we are humbled to allow the spirit of God to work through us even more for His purpose. Remember our walk and gifts are not about us but for us to be a servant unto the Lord. So, allow yourselves to become weak in Him. He is there to make us strong.

Servant hood: (Matt 20: 25-28)

Great leaders are the ones who are great at servant hood. When God is taking you through this process, He is making a leader out of you. You must become a servant in order to become a leader. You must show yourself worthy in this season. Give one who is a servant at heart a position of authority and they will not misuse it, but use it to serve others. The meek shall inherit the Earth.

Meekness (Matt 5:5)

If we must force or prove our leadership on others, we show that we are not leaders. A wise leader is peaceable and easily entreated (James 3; 17). The school of character that God takes a prophet through occurs in the school of everyday life. This training is more than any secular classroom or teaching can ever provide. Prophets must be very careful not to allow their gift(s) to go to their head during the process of birthing forth their ministry. If they are not careful, it will lead to their demise. This is the reason why the training must be so intense. Just like school, if you don't meet the requirements to pass the first time, you will have to repeat it again. As it is in the natural so it is in the spirit.

The following scriptures will provide purpose and understanding.

(Hebrew 12:11)
Now no chastening seems to be joyful for the present, but painful. Nevertheless, afterward it yields the peaceable fruit of righteousness to those who have been trained by it.

(2 Cor 4: 7, 17, 18)
7. But we have this treasure in earthen vessels that the excellence of the power may be of God and not us.
17. For our light afflictions, which is but for a moment, are working for us a far more exceeding and eternal weight of glory.
18. While we do not look at the things which are seen, but at the things which are not seen: for the things which are seen are temporal; but the things which are not seen are eternal.

The way the Lord talks

We have a Father God that is a communicating God. He loves to talk to His children and He wants each one of us to know how to hear His voice clearly and accurately. God doesn't have any favorites. He desires to speak to each one of us. He desires to meet with us in our everyday lives and speak to us about our day to day activities. If you are a child of God, born again and filled with the Holy Spirit, you should be able to hear the voice of God speaking to you. You do not need to be a prophet you just need to be a son. You have been adopted into the family you must develop a relationship with the Father. This is a normal part of our salvation in Christ Jesus. God expects you to draw nigh, so He can whisper or speak audibly in your ear.

In order to recognize and hear the voice of God clearly and with accuracy, you must go through a learning process. Those of us that can hear the voice of the Lord can probably remember the first time you may have heard His voice. Although you may not be able to decipher His voice, God is so interested in communication with His children that He begins to speak to us on a regular basis even before we learn how to discern His voice. This is to help some recognize the areas where God has already spoken to them. Hopefully, this will motivate them even more to listen for the voice of God, so they can hear Him more accurately in every area of their lives.

Other ways God speaks and leads us

The following are different ways the Lord communicates with us

- *Through scripture and the quickening of portions of scripture*

- *Seeing object lessons*

- *Divine Coincidences*

- *Internal prompting*

- *Visions and Dreams*

- *Checks in our spirits*

- *Conviction of the Holy Spirit (He is our umpire)*

- *Hearing something and getting an inner witness*

- *Angels*

The Language of the prophet

God speaks to his prophet in many ways. In this, the prophet can see pictures, visions, and/or dreams. He also can get things in his senses of smell, taste, or feelings. When God uses the prophet to prophesy to someone, He gives the prophet some of these things. The prophet/prophetic person will usually hear the Voice of God in their thoughts, senses, or through the prompting of the Holy Spirit.

In the Old Testament, the Urim and Thummim were given to the high priest to use for getting direction from God. These were stones which gave direction and counsel to Israel when it was needed. They were objects kept in a bag of the breastplate and often used in a flow of the prophetic. God's way of speaking is not our way. In order to understand His way, it's imperative that we tap into the realm of the spirit. (Isaiah 55:8) "My thoughts are not your thoughts and my ways are not your ways declares the Lord." It is vitally important to learn the way prophecy comes. Some of the teachings are actually hidden in the meaning of different

Hebrew and Aramaic root words translated in our English text for prophecy. They have a wealth of expression and actually describe the way in which God's inspiration comes. Two of the words, Ro'eh and Chozeh, underline the passive experience of receiving the prophetic message from God. While the other three words, Massa, Naba and Nataf, describe the active experience of communicating God's message to the audience.

RO'EH

The word Ro'eh literally means "a seer" and occurs 12 times in the Hebrew text of the Old Testament. The word describes distinctively the prophetic revelation of the prophet through visions.

CHOZEH

Is also another translated word in our English Bible as 'prophet' Chozeh carries a base Hebrew meaning of "a seer" this word is used 26 times in the Hebrew text. This prophet receives communication from God more from visions and dreams then audible words. The chozeh's experiences and spiritual receptions are applied under the prophet's anointing. Prophets who say they saw the word of the Lord more than heard it are examples of this type of prophet.

MASSA

The Hebrew term "Massa" and its root, Nassah, are used 70 times in the Old Testament. Its prophetic meaning is a "burden" and reveals the response of the one receiving God's message. It comes like a weight or burden upon the prophet. (Is 13:23) and one after another the burden of the Lord came upon Isaiah as he spoke God's word of rebuke and judgment over Babylon. Jeremiah, known as a weeping prophet, experienced the weight of the word in his bowels. Massa is also defined as the lifting up of the soul in the prophetic flow of the temple musicians as exemplified in the master musician Chenaniah who was the master of song.

NABA

This Aramaic and Hebrew word "Naba" means to "bubble up", to gush or pour forth. Recorded in the Old Testament over 435 times, the word of God flows from the inner most part of our being as a river of life. (Amos 3:8) the Sovereign Lord has spoken, who can but "Naba" prophesy. (Joel 2:28) your sons and your daughters shall "Naba" prophesy.

NATAF

Here is the second Hebrew word for prophecy that is used to describe the communication dynamic. The prophetic message is an interplay between the reception of God's words and the giving of those words through a human vessel. While Naba describes the communication of a prophetic word that bubbles up from within, Nataf pictures a flow of words that actually drop *upon the messenger as drops of rain. Just as you wait for rain to fall, so must a prophet wait on the words to be streamed from God. He gives you a set of words then you are waiting on the other words like rain falling from Heaven.*

The Language of the Prophet

God uses a variety of different ways to communicate prophetically to His people. Those who have been called to the office particularly, have a rough training or preparation. Because of the intensity of the training, it is imperative that a prophet/prophetic person understand the methods of language so he or she can properly serve God and flow in his or her call.

These methods include:

- *The spirit of prophecy*
- *The Gift of Prophecy*
- *Prophetic Presbytery*
- *Prophetic preaching*
- *The Office of the Prophet*

The Spirit of Prophecy

There are times during corporate worship where God's Spirit is present to communicate His heart to His people. During this time, a special anointing for a prophetic word is released to any member of that group. We must understand the release of the prophetic anointing is not related to a person's office or gifting. It is according to how you avail yourself to the Holy Spirit's flow. If you are indeed in a prophetic setting, all can prophesy as you are willing to step out on faith. 1 Cor. 14:26-33 speaks of coming together in a corporate worship setting singing and preaching. The exercise of spiritual gifts and prophesy is a chief motivator in this type of service. As we come together, these gifts edify and strengthen other believers. This is called a spirit of prophecy.

The Bible gives several examples of the spirit of Prophecy. In 1 Samuel 10:10 & 11, a prophet is someone who speaks God's words. God told many prophets to predict certain events. What God wanted most was for them to instruct and inspire people to live in faithfulness to God. When Saul's colleagues heard the prophetic words coming from Saul, they exclaimed "is Saul among the prophets?" So the question is: was he now a prophet? As you may see, he was around the office (company of) prophets. The spirit of prophecy fell upon him.

The Gift of Prophecy

The gift of prophecy is just that. It's one of the gifts of the Holy Spirit. It is given to those whom God chooses. It is not based on merit. It is based upon the grace of God. However, scripture gives us some indication that if we earnestly desire and ask God for the gift, through faith He will give it.

(1 Corinthians 14:1 AMP) 14 eagerly pursue and seek to acquire [this] love [make it your aim, your great quest]; and earnestly desire and cultivate the spiritual endowments (gifts), especially that you may prophesy ([a]interpret the divine will and purpose in inspired preaching and teaching).

(Romans 12:6 (AMP) 6 having gifts (faculties, talents, qualities) that differ according to the grace given us, let us use them: [He whose gift is] prophecy, [let him prophesy] according to the proportion of his faith;

(Galatians AMP)5 Then does He Who supplies you with His marvelous [Holy] Spirit and works powerfully and miraculously among you, do so on [the grounds of your doing] what the Law demands, or because of your believing in and adhering to and trusting in and relying on the message that you heard?

The Gift of Prophecy is listed among the nine gifts of the Holy Spirit in 1 Corinthians Chapter 12. Its purpose is to edify, exhort, and comfort. Not only does it bring the believer to a place in God but it also convicts and transforms the unbeliever.

(1Cor. 14:3 AMP) But [on the other hand], the one who prophesies [who [a]interprets the divine will and purpose in inspired preaching and teaching] speaks to men for their up building and constructive spiritual progress and encouragement and consolation.

Prophetic Preaching

There is a difference between preaching and prophesying. Prophecy is usually the spontaneous revelation knowledge inspired by the Holy Spirit. Preaching is the speaking of The Logos (written word), while prophecy gives a rhema (fresh breath of revelation) from the Spirit of God. Although different, there are times when the Holy Spirit will move on a prepared teaching and modify it by breathing a dimension of life/inspiration into it. When this happens, the Holy Spirit generally ends up changing the message of the preparer. In order to preach a prophetic sermon, it requires both proper preparation and openness to allow the Holy Spirit to change the agenda.

Prophetic preaching has the following Characteristics

- It has biblical truth. All prophetic messages should line up to the written word of God.
- The symbolization and examples used by God are precise to communicate to His people. God

selects Illustrations that directly pierce the heart of the people in the room.

- *The hearer will have the impression that God is talking directly to him/her.*
- *You don't need to be a prophet for God to use you in prophetic preaching.*
- *The message is targeted specifically for the people who are present at the time.*
- *Prophetic preaching is typically delivered by someone who holds one of the fivefold offices Prophet, Pastor, Apostle, Teacher and Evangelist.*

The Office of the Prophet

As we have discussed previously, the ministry of a prophet is not a gift of the Holy Spirit available to all believers. It is an office that Jesus put in place-an extension of His government over the church. As we know, the office of the prophet is one of five headship ministries.
(Eph 2:20AMP) *²⁰ you are built upon the foundation of the apostles and prophets with Christ Jesus Himself the chief Cornerstone.*
Offices are not gifts they are governmental positions. Christ selects and places certain individuals into governmental leadership in the body and gifts them accordingly. Jesus Christ was the complete manifestation and our perfect example of all fivefold ministry offices.

Biblical Basics for the office
Jesus the Apostle-
- **Hebrews 3:1** *(AMP)*
  3 So then, brethren, consecrated and set apart for God, who share in the heavenly calling, [thoughtfully and attentively] consider Jesus, the Apostle and High Priest Whom we confessed [as ours when we embraced the Christian faith].

Jesus the Prophet-
- **Acts 3:22** *(AMP)*
  ²² Thus Moses said to the forefathers, The Lord God will raise up for you a Prophet from among your brethren as [He raised up] me; Him you shall listen to and understand by hearing and heed in all things whatever He tells you.

Jesus the Evangelist-
- **Matthew 4:23** *(AMP)*
  ²³ and He went about all Galilee, teaching in their synagogues and preaching the good news (Gospel) of the kingdom, and healing every disease and every weakness and infirmity among the people.

Jesus the Pastor-
- **John 10:14** *(AMP)*
  ¹⁴ I am the Good Shepherd; and I know and recognize my own, and my own know and recognize me—

Jesus the Teacher-
- *John 3:2 (AMP)*
  ²Who came to Jesus at night and said to Him, Rabbi, we know and are certain that You have come from God [as] a Teacher; for no one can do these signs (these wonderworks, these miracles—and produce the proofs) that You do unless God is with him.
  After Christ ascended into heaven, the five ministries Jesus embodied on Earth were given back to the church and to His people who were called to fulfill the office. According to Ephesians 4:11 all the offices are distributed and should be moving in full maturation. The mantle enabled Christ to be the Great Apostle of faith was given to those chosen by Jesus to be Apostles. Likewise, Jesus' evangelistic anointing is given to the Evangelist, the Pastor receives the heart and the staff of the good Sheppard, and the Teacher is given Jesus' divine ability to teach. Those chosen to be New Testament Prophets receive the qualities and ability to know what's in the hearts of God's people and to announce His purpose, secrets, and future plans.

Now the Office of the Prophet

According to 1 Corinthians 14:3 & 4, the gift of prophecy is for three main functions: edification, exhortation, and comfort. However, the Office of the Prophet is designed and has authority invested in a mantle to function in a higher realm and sphere of ministry than the Holy Spirit's Gift of Prophecy.

The Importance of Development

In this part of the lesson we will go over the gift, the ministry and the office. If you can imagine a pool and in it has a low, shallow end a middle, and a higher end in its levels of depth. At the shallow end, there is a mixture of our thoughts competing with the mind of the spirit of God. As we receive proper training and discipleship and opportunity to move in the gift, we develop our listening ability, we learn to filter out our own thoughts, discern the voice of the enemy and hold fast to the word of God. In the prophetic ministry there is less mixture; we are growing into the gift and establishing credibility and a good track record. Most times once you notice how the gift works, it will be a time for God putting it on a shelf and putting the prophetic person on the potter's wheel to be made. As we move into the prophetic office, we come into a greater flow of revelatory anointing and responsibility on the national and international scenes. All ministries must grow; if we halt our development our ministry will hit a ceiling and level off. This will continue to happen if we don't allow God to put the gift on the shelf and the prophet willingly gets on the wheel so the potter can make the person. Without adequate training our gifting will not reach beyond a certain level. The fivefold ministry gifts(Ephesians 4:11) of Apostles, prophets, evangelist, pastors and teachers have their main function to (equip) the saints for service(Ephesians 4:12) there are varying kinds of prophets with different types of anointing it is the same with church leadership there are different anointing's and ministry's so everyone is not going to act the same. The most important thing to learn is how to rule in the specific sphere of influence.

The Prophetic Ministry

After the shallow end, in the spirit there is a middle section where the waters start to get deeper. In prophecy there are times when you must push in deeper expressing the heart of God. Prophetic ministry is quite different from the gift of prophecy, many people will experience prophecy as a onetime gift for a particular time and purpose. Prophecy can supply specific details to general principles. For example the bible can tell us how to live but not instructions on were to live. It tells us how to meet together but not the specific location of the church meeting. When we talk about prophetic ministry, it goes into different spheres this can be prophetic intercession, singing prophetically, prophetic words or prophetic preaching, or giving a direction and instruction to a church. The prophetic ministry is concerned with the church and what direction the church is going. Each church and ministry has times of testing's battles to fight and things to overcome. Prophetic ministry brings God's perspective, Releases vision and calling and undermines the enemy. It is concerned in seeing the church fulfill its call. It draws attention to the majesty and supremacy of God in times of trouble. It has one hand in the past and one hand in the future. But is able to bring elements into the present to help us make sense of what we are going through. Prophetic ministry see the continuity of Gods purpose from our past to our future. The knowledge of both these things helps us to come to the conclusion of the reality of the matter. This prophetic perspective ignites faith and hope and gives us the energy to fight the good fight and break through.

The office of A Prophet

The office of a prophet would continue along the same lines, but going even deeper into the supernatural realm of hearing God and being his mouth piece; the prophet is concerned with holiness and purity and is seeking to prepare the bride of Christ. The end time theme will be the utmost important as they build the church and establish kingdom values and practices for Christ's return. The office has a kingdom perspective that will motivate the church universal towards a practical unity of the spirit. The office prophet will speak to churches, cities, regions and nations God's word will be heard to all in authority: church leaders, kings, and governments. God's words will be accompanied by signs and wonders in healing and deliverance signs and wonders.

Introduction of Prophetic Intercession
Daniel chapters 9:20-23 ~ 10:10-13 ~ Luke: 2:36-38

Intercession: *Intervening on another's behalf by interposing oneself between two parties and their difficulties or crises, usually by prayer but also by means of aid. Arbitration or mediation.*

Prophetic Intercession: *The term for the peculiar high powered prayers of prophets whereby revelatory insight, historical experience, and official authority unite to cause the petition of the prophet to be granted by God. Once heard, the words they utter take on the effects of altering static situations and conditions that others may have no effect upon. Prophetic Intercession involves prayer, declarations, commands and decrees and various supernatural executive or legislative acts prophets are authorized by the Lord to influence.*
These official actions on behalf of the most high compel the holds of darkness to release themselves from their captives, objects and their possessions. Prophetic Intercession involves the prophet's intervention, interruption, interposition and interjection of the will, word, and works of God in a human situation or earthly affair. In a word, the prophet's intercession licenses the power, authority and sovereignty of the Lord to be exercised by them. In Jeremiah 15:1; Moses and Samuel were commemorated by God as the earliest standard of prophetic intercession. Besides them are Daniel who served the most high God.

As has been often heard, all prophets are intercessors but not all intercessors are prophets. I would venture to say that not all intercessors are even prophetic intercessors, but many are. Prayer is the basis for every ministry, but some have the unique gift from God for praying. Intercessors are usually very quiet and low key personalities, but forceful in their prayer times. They are even a little "strange" to the general public, hearing things and feeling needs that most others don't - at least not in the measure that they hear and feel them. Intercessors will take a need or a word and rehearse it and rehearse it before the Lord, often using Scriptures to back up the request in asking God to honor His Word. They understand certain things that please His Heart and appeal to that. They know how to knock and keep on knocking. It's a gift, subject to the will of God.
Prophets on the other hand love to pray but their prayer styles are different. Prophets are visionaries. Not only do they see and assess the status quo, they see the needs and desire for positive change. As a prophet matures, they will see many options in the plan of God. They can

become so burdened for the needs that many are called judgment prophets for a season because they are so zealous to see God act.

Many in their zeal get ahead of God and man and declare their wishes as the plan when it is only a possibility in the making. A prophet, as a friend of God, walks with God and has insight but can forget the free will that God has given man. God does not reveal all of His omnipotent knowledge to any mortal, but the little that He does release can so impress some that they believe the prophet "knows everything." They don't, but if they walk with God and pay the price to do that, they do get to know His heart and mind and share a portion of His supernatural insight. When we walk in the Light as He is in the Light, the dark things are exposed. But as that begins to happen, the individual must focus to have the heart that Jesus did and that is to motivate and redeem people to leave the darkness and come into the Light of His Life.

Intercessors have a special ministry gift that others don't, either in capacity or ability. Every minister must intercede as Jesus for the people they minister to, but intercessors put oil on the wheels. We each have a personal gift of prayer for the working out of our individual calling. No one can steal that, or do that work for you. But when it comes to the Body working as a whole, the intercessors carry a key role. It's easy to overlook. It's easy to believe that our own prayers are sufficient for the works of God, but our eyes need to be unveiled to this truth. Many people think, "Oh how nice, you prayed." And they take it as a compliment that you prayed for them or that you did something for self-improvement or that you genuinely cared or were just whiling away the time in a "comfortable" activity. Many do not understand the spiritual forces at work.

Intercession is a servant gift. When Jesus prayed, He prayed for the will of the Father. He worked to do what the Father was doing. He intercedes for mankind - even to the point that He laid down His earthly life for us. Intercessors are close to the Father's heart. They follow direction. Now prophets are seers who make the vision plain so that others may run with it. They don't have the all-knowing mind of God but they have portions of it released to them. God releases a word by His Spirit and the prophets pick up the sound of His Voice and put it into human words. With good and Godly people skills, they convey the messages and other ministers work with that as well.

One think a prophetic Intercessor or prophet must learn and understand is spiritual warfare. Spiritual warfare is a tool, armor used by the servant to know his or her enemies and or allies. The intercessor must know how Satan's kingdom operates and know it has a cosmological system. (Quotations come from the rules of engagement.) The word cosmology speaks of the dynamic arrangement of the universe and the world. God created the world in an orderly fashion. Satan has created a perverted imitation of it. By using such people as Cain and other rebellious men as pawns, he has successfully constructed a world that in reality is nothing more than just a great magic show with illusions, smoke and mirrors to fool the blinded eyes of man. People of God it is paramount that we see after the father in this time to see what he is saying to us about intercession. (Gen 4:9-24). In this particular portion of scripture, we see the terrestrial foundation of the kingdom of darkness taking shape and form through the creation of eight out of the twelve existing systems that comprise our world:

1.   Social system (culture, language, marriage and family)
2.   Entertainment
3.   Environmental
4.   Economical
5.   Governmental
6.   Educational
7.   Technological
8.   Religious (humanistic, atheistic, and anti-God)

These systems, originally designed by God to provide the optimum environment for mankind to fulfill its purpose and maximize potential, and to reach its destiny, have now become the strongholds of demonic forces. Today we can witness the effects of the presence of the enemy in this world. Governments are corrupt, approximately half of all marriages end in divorce, we have same sex marriage laws, and families that once were secure and safe are now plagued with perversions, abuse, dysfunction, and violence, leaving our educational systems in need. Our environmental system has been in a bad place from sin, sickness, contamination and disease. Our religious system is at an all- time high of apostasy, idol worship and delusion. And rejection of the true and living God.

As Prophetic Intercessors you need these key quality things:

1.   A relationship with God (prayer life) that is consistent
2.   Life of sacrifice and consecration
3.   Prophetic Discernment (Prophetic Instincts, prophetic Sensations,)
4.   Learn and understand Spiritual warfare
5.   How to use your weapons and know who your enemies are and how to fight against your enemies.

The Kingdom of Darkness is an Elaborately Organized Kingdom: The Kingdom of darkness is well equipped and very ready to fight a pitched battle using any and all means at its disposal. Remember, you are engaged in a battle with a very organized system of protocol and chain command. The following is a description of the kingdom of darkness. You are a general in the *spirit so you must understand how the demonic generals work.*

1.   *Principalities: The word principality comes from the Greek word achromatic which, literally translated means first in rank and order. Principalities derive their power directly from Satan and are the highest ranking entities in Satan's army. They influence the affairs of humanity at a national level, impacting laws and policies. They are so purpose specific that they often embody world leaders.*

2.   *Powers: Next in the chain of command we find powers, the Greek word for power, exousia speaks of delegated authority. These are demonic spirits that derive their jurisdictional and delegated authority from principalities. They affect and infect structures, systems and the five pillars of our society: marriage, family, government, education and church.*

3.   *Rulers of darkness of this world: Kosmokrator and skoto, are the Greek words used for this category of spirits. These spirits are very high ranking officers that have specialized jurisdiction over the twelve cosmological systems of the universe and rule in the kingdom of darkness. They are responsible for blinding the minds of the people to truth and for facilitating sin, wickedness and iniquity within the nations of the world. They are also responsible for keeping people in a state of darkness; I am not merely speaking of the absence of light, but of the absence of God. They affect the thoughts, feelings, and perceptions of humanity through mass media, music, movies, fashion, sports, philosophies and religious ideologies.*

4.   *Spiritual wickedness in high places: the Greek phrase pneumatikos poneria epouranios Speaks of types of spirits found in high and lofty places that are responsible for anything that is perverted, depraved, debased, warped or corrupt. This spirit is spoken of as working from high, lofty, and heavenly places that speak of not only celestial zones and dimensions but also the mind. Which is a type of a heavenly place? It influences, seduces and falsely inspires actions, perceptions motivations, fantasies, imaginations and appetites through the overt or convert attack and influence of the mind, affecting terrestrial and celestial domains. According to Daniel these spirits operation in the second heaven, frustrate and prohibit the manifestation and answers to believer's prayers. Perceptions, mindsets, paradigms, ideologies, and belief systems are twisted and perverted to accommodate the personality of these evil spirits.*

5.   *Devils and demons: Literally translated from the Greek word daimonion, demon means distributor of fortunes. A demon or devil is a supernatural spirit that possesses the nature of Satan and has the ability to give and distribute fortunes Mammon of the unrighteous, possess man, and control mindsets and activities. Devils can be worshiped, make people sick communicate, and involve themselves in host of other diabolical activities.*

6.   *Spirits of the underworld: these sprits work with high witchcraft operations the underworld has six regions, and none of which are places you would not ever want to go.*

- *Death ~ (1 Cor 15-55; Job 34:22)*
- *Hell/Sheol/Hades ~ (Isa 14:19)*
- *The grave (Isa 38:10; Ezek 31:15)*
- *The Pit (Ezek 32:23)*
- *The abyss ~ the lower region of the pit (Isa 38:17; Ps 30:3)*
- *Regions of the sea (Job 41:1-31; Ezek 26:16)*

Now that you can recognize you have an enemy and can combat him, here are some things you must understand.

1. Prophetic Discernment: the ability of the prophet to detect manifestations, influences, and apparitions or psycho-emotional conditions normally unseen or overlooked by non-prophetic types.
Prophetic discernments a cultivated gift that relies on experience, exposure to a wide range of prophetic and insight into a breath of human situations, collectively, these facilitate the active and accurate exercise of prophetic ministry. 1 Cor 12:10, one of the gifts of the spirit it apparently refers to the God giving ability to tell whether a prophetic speech came from Gods spirit or from another source opposed to God. -1John 4: 1-6- Hebrews 5; 12-14

2. Prophetic Instincts: Special faculties inherent in certain people where they sense, perceive, and can identify what is happening behind the veil of this world. This faculty is available to all who have the Holy Spirit. Along with sensing the events, those that have this faculty understand its prophetic factions, Objectives and manifestations. These can also discern weather this event or action is or is not of God. Also sensing the presence of a prophet's spirit in a person, or recognizing the shifts of the Lord from one stream to another.

3. Prophetic Sensations: the term for the diverse physical and physiological experiences felt by the prophet in preparation for duty. The sensations were felt by Jeremiah the prophet and touched his human emotions, feelings, and discomforts. They include the weighty hand of the Lord resting upon them uncomfortably until a prophetic task is completed.

4. Delusion: Error in strategy and its effects of falsehood and mockery for the purpose of deception and seduction. 2 Thess 2:10-12, John 4:6

Some other things you must know as a prophetic Intercessor.

In addition, to understanding your position as a prophetic intercessor; to know that God is going to deal with you also in dreams and visions. God dealt with Daniel in dreams and visions and also had given him the mantle of interpretation. In this God allows the prophetic person access to realms and spheres they did not have before. It can get quite frustrating what is a dream or just a vision; information to speak forth or information to intercede about. First and for most all what is seen must be prayed about before you move forward on any of these things. These Gifts must be cultivated by exercise and exposure; to prophetic situations. These all come forth as parables, signs, symbols, manifestations, (taste, smell, and feelings).which sometimes the prophetic person cannot understand in the carnal realm. Prophets are groomed for ministry through parables and symbols. (See Ezekiel) This is a good reason most prophetic people need a prophetic mentor; for prophetic Activation, Apprenticeship and covering.

Interpretation: Explaining difficult thought, teachings, information in terms that hears can easily understand. Making the vague and cryptic clear. Defining what a message sender actually meant or intended by the message sent.

Prophetic Guard: The term given for the shield of spiritual force that prophets emit to deflect the assaults and stratagems devils throw at the people of God. This is very vital to the local church. Prophetic Guards pray, intercede, compel provision manifestation, and enforce obedience upon the forces of darkness.

Seer: one who sees in the spirit realm and prophesies what is seen.
Samuel judged Israel and was called a seer early in his ministry. A Seers gestures can mimic other spiritual activities that somewhat mirror and official prophet. Seers' manifestations may also be observed in strong intercessors.

Seeing Prophets: An oversight prophet who receives his or her communication from God mostly through visions and dreams. A seeing prophet's mantle has strong Shepard ship, and Pastoral elements attached.

Spiritual Mantel's
Scripture reference: 1 Kings 19:19-21 and 2 Kings 2:13-15

Definitions

Mantle: *(natural) A loose fitting garment worn by prophets and other officials in authority to signify their position and power to exercise dominion. Mantles reflect latitude, stature. Prestige and provisions of the wearer, as well as the license to act and operate.*

Mantle Treatment: what is learned, practiced, supplied to, and provided for the mantle of ministers to equip and empower them for service to the Lord. These are beyond normal church services and believers bible studies, Mentorship and school of ministry is needed especially for the prophet and the Apostle. Ministry apprenticeship is needed for effective treating ones mantle.

Prophetic Office: The Position of Trust and authority bestowed upon prophets/prophetess to install them as agents and functionaries of The Most High God.

Prophetic Officiations: The term used to identify a prophets/prophetess execution of the office on behalf of God.

Prophetic Realm: The realm of ministry a prophet/Prophetess class of service consistently and most successfully fits within. Realms speak more to physical locales, territories over which the prophetic has jurisdiction. Churches, ministries and business situated in strategic zones throughout the earth are what is meant.

Prophetic Sphere: The area of human life or earthly affairs God assigns a prophet to, in addition to its counterpart in the realm of the church. Prophetic spheres are evidenced by the consistent yet distinctive success of the routine activity most emphasized in a prophet/prophetess ministry experiences. It is where a prophet's angelic delegation operates and propels the prophet's mantle to overpower, treat, or provoke more than anything else. The demonstrations of the Holy Spirit manifest themselves in these spheres of existence on the prophet's behalf most consistently. Marriage, religion, business, youth, entertainment military or politics are all examples of the spheres to which the prophet may be assigned.

Prophetic Incubation: A term to describe the season of separation and often isolation whereby divine messengers are groomed for service by God. Prophetic Incubation is where the spirit of the prophet is awakened to the calling and filled with the elements for the ministry. In the past incubation took place in caves or similar dwellings most times sent to the wilderness for the same purpose.

Prophetic Mantle: the term of the cloak (spiritually speaking) worn by prophets to designate their authority in their ministry community and in the spirit realm. John the Baptist, Elijah, and many other prophets were recognized by the unique style of mantle they wore. The old mantles were generally made of camel's hair and were gathered at the waist with a wide leather belt. Today the prophet's mantle carries with it the same powers without the need to dress so differently on the outside the purpose it serves today is more for the invisible agents of God's creation than for the people of earth. The mantles of the prophet signify to them the status, authority, and station of the officer in the prophetic realms of creation.

You cannot receive a mantle until you have a prophetic incubation season in your prophetic walk. Once there, the only life the novice encounters is the deity of GOD orienting the prophet for prophetic service. Visions, dreams, inner conflicts and wrestling's with the opposers of their mantles occupy the novices time in incubation. During this time they are expected to confront and conquer every fear, inhibition, or resistance arising to resist who and what they are called to become.

The idea of prophetic incubation is that the prophet would learn the ways of the spiritual world and the means by which he or she would bring forth prophecy, oracles, and supernatural emanations of all kind. Getting familiar with the invisible spheres of creation and the higher unseen powers of the land, as well as confidence in receiving and understanding the messages therefore are what the incubation season is to bring about.(John the Baptist, Elijah) all underwent prophetic incubation.

Also when dealing with the prophetic mantle there is prophetic mantle treatment, and prophetic competence, which is the status and conditions of a prophets skill in relation to the task and requirements of the office. The meaning includes the prophets conflict with the spiritual and carnal resistance to the word of the Lord from him or her and his her ability to overcome them. (See Elisha's early Ministry in 2 Kings). Mantles~ were important articles of clothing they represent protection, anointing and representation of authority and power in the spirit. In this Elijah put his mantle on Elisha to represent him becoming his predecessor/ successor which is to succeed one in office or position.

Elijah: was a complex man of the desert who counseled Kings. As we know Mt Carmel was his greatest public miracle, his prophetic role, anointing constantly placed him in opposition to the Majority. Prophetic Mantles carry: Miracles, signs, wonders, healing and deliverance also a power to change and shift.

Elisha: was Elijah's prodigy, predecessor, and mentoree, he did greater exploits then his Mentor. Striking the water proved his attachment to the mantle. We cannot just take other peoples mantles and think we can use them those that know who the chief prophet is (Demons/Angels) in high places. Will not recognize you. Mantles just won't work with anyone. But those who have been chosen and appointed for them this is why there were witnesses from the school of the prophets. Prophets can carry multiple mantles.

PROPHETIC MENTORSHIP
Matthew 4:18-22; Isaiah 54:13, 14; 1 Kings 19:16-21

Prophetic Mentorship: An essential term for the prophet's sphere of training and preparation. It explains the novice prophet who voluntarily submits to a Chief Prophet or an Apostle for the purposes of training, cultivation, and eventually God's use. Elisha and Elijah are biblical examples of this vital prophetic custom.

Mentor: One, who coaches, instructs and refines another for a professional career or service.

Mentoree: the student or prodigy of the mentor.

Mentor Manipulation: Negative behavior, conduct and attitudes that mistreat a mentoree by one trusted with their professional development and grooming. Misuse of mentor authority to the personal advantage of the tutor that damages, or subverts their training and preparation. Extreme hardship abuse and neglect or oppression applied by the mentor to a learner in the quise of preparatory enrichment. Servitude demanded by one expected to equip another for future service that is unrealistic and unreasonable in comparison to its potential rewards and future opportunities.

Prophetic Apprenticeship: The term that describes the tenure of a prophet in training. It takes under a seasoned prophet's oversight for development, training, refinement and accreditation of the novice's mantle. Elisha, Joshua, and the 12 apostles all completed prophetic apprenticeship.

Jesus Christ the perfect Mentor: *Matthew 4:18-22;* *18*
As He was walking by the Sea of Galilee, He noticed two brothers, Simon who is called Peter and Andrew his brother, throwing a dragnet into the sea, for they were fishermen.
19 And He said to them, Come [ ]after me [as disciples—letting me be your Guide], follow me, and I will make you fishers of men!
20 At once they left their nets and [ ]became His disciples [sided with His party and followed Him]. 21 And going on further from there He noticed two other brothers, James son of Zebedee and his brother John, in the boat with their father Zebedee, mending their nets and putting them right; and He called them. 22 At once they left the boat and their father and [ ]joined Jesus as disciples [sided with His party and followed Him].

Isaiah: 54:13; 14 13 and all your [spiritual] children shall be disciples [taught by the Lord and obedient to His will], and great shall be the peace and undisturbed composure of your children. 14 You shall establish yourself in righteousness (rightness, in conformity with God's will and order): you shall be far from even the thought of oppression or destruction, for you shall not fear, and from terror, for it shall not come near you.

The Great Prophetic Mentor: *1Kings 19:16-21*

16 And anoint Jehu son of Nimshi to be king over Israel, and anoint Elisha son of Shaphat of Abel-meholah to be prophet in your place. 17 And him who escapes from the sword of Hazael Jehu shall slay, and him who escapes the sword of Jehu Elisha shall slay.
18 Yet I will leave myself 7,000 in Israel, all the knees that have not bowed to Baal and every mouth that has not kissed him. 19 So Elijah left there and found Elisha son of Shaphat, whose plowing was being done with twelve yoke of oxen, and he drove the twelfth. Elijah crossed over to him and cast his mantle upon him. 20 He left the oxen and ran after Elijah and said, let me kiss my father and mother, and then I will follow you. And he [testing Elisha] said, Go on back. What have I done to you? [Settle it for yourself.] 21 So Elisha went back from him. Then he took a yoke of oxen, slew them, boiled their flesh with the oxen's yoke [as fuel], and gave to the people, and they ate. Then he arose, followed Elijah, and served him.

What to Expect From Mentorship/the Facts of Mentorship

Mentorship can be integral for all creation. Mentorship is a function, mentors should be educated in the area or field of ministry their entrée's are called and are in need of mentoring. Prophet's especially need to be mentored. Mentorship's are to be mutually rewarding and mutually cooperative arrangements. Mentoree's should expect to have scheduled training, sessions of lectures, and development. And be required to attend them. Mentor assignments should look to practice ministry functions & outlets. Mentorship relies on integrity, devotion, diligence, and loyalty. Mentorship must be formed with clear and honest motives & well defined objectives. Undeclared objectives & outcomes endanger the success of any mentorship.

Prophetic Mentorship: An essential term for the prophet's sphere of training and preparation. It explains the novice prophet who voluntarily submits to a Chief Prophet or an Apostle for the purposes of training, cultivation, and eventually God's use. Elisha and Elijah are biblical examples of this vital prophetic custom.

Mentor: One, who coaches, instructs and refines another for a professional career or service.

Mentoree: the student or prodigy of the mentor.

Mentor Manipulation: Negative behavior, conduct and attitudes that mistreat a mentoree by one trusted with their professional development and grooming. Misuse of mentor authority to the personal advantage of the tutor that damages, or subverts their training and preparation. Extreme hardship abuse and neglect or oppression applied by the mentor to a learner in the guise of preparatory enrichment. Servitude demanded by one expected to equip another for future service that is unrealistic and unreasonable in comparison to its potential rewards and future opportunities.

Prophetic Apprenticeship: The term that describes the tenure of a prophet in training. It takes under a seasoned prophet's oversight for development, training, refinement and accreditation of the novice's mantle. Elisha, Joshua, and the 12 apostles all completed prophetic apprenticeship.

People of God in this dispensation and time the body of Christ is in hard places, of deception and the state of delusion and need to be alert and aware of what posture our God in putting us in. We will have many mentors, and many that will counsel you. But you will only have one father and Mother (spiritual). We need to understand God is positioning us to make disciples of men and women and what you may possess is not for you alone but to give out to others, not to your own judgment of what you may perceive they may or may not have or need to receive. You don't know who the next Elijah or Elisha, Or John the Baptist, or Samuel or Daniel, God will allow you to impart into and help make a great warrior in God. May the Lord bless you all in this endeavor to become all God wants you to become.

Mentoring describes a process of developing a man or woman to his/ her maximum potential in Jesus Christ. Mentors serve various functions, role model healthy, Biblical, holy lifestyles. Supervise & provide pastoral spiritual direction on Christian goal management. Provide individualized Christian help & encouragement based on the unique purposes, gifts, and calling of each mentee. Encourage and support growth areas in the mentee, confront & challenge thoughts, behaviors and actions which do not line up with Godly sense of purpose for the mentee's life and the stated mentoring goals. Assist the mentee in actively thinking, speaking, and behaving in new life giving ways consistent with healthy righteous priorities and values. Provide practical spiritual biblical direction on how to draw out potential that may have been dormant.

Prophetic Mentorship

For those called in the prophetic ministry, the beginnings and early development stages can be frustrating, lonely, discouraging and can be a confusing time. It helps to have a support network of brothers and sisters who are like minded. Mentoring fathers in the faith is an important ingredient in raising a prophetic generation that is balanced, holy and healthy for the body of Christ. We need mentors in our lives. Sadly now days we have lost the concept of mentorship. There are very few who are even willing to rise up and mentor or who would be considered healthy role models to do so. Instead if asked many who would long to have this mentorship have only had tormentors. Prophetic people need a lot of mentor- ship and love and understanding.

NEXT PHASE ~ IN MENTORSHIP

Our vision is that this prophetic ministry and movement will become a spiritual boot camp and a training forum to raise an Army. We want to usher you into a new level of understanding of your prophetic calling. This can be done as we mentor mature relationships one with another into new levels of mature leadership. This prophetic army and warrior bride will receive a double portion of God's anointing and a deeper understanding of intimacy with the Lord JESUS because of a revelation and understanding of mentorship through divinely appointed relationships. This grace will usher you by the mercy of God through the Holy Spirit into a divinely appointed mentoring relationship just for you.

In our prophetic ministry experience and journey, just like Paul begetting Timothy and Elijah begetting Elisha, we would like to raise sons and daughters in Christ. You can only reproduce what you are. The prophetic remnants can only give birth to the same. I pray that God will meet us at the anointed level in him and usher us into deep levels of mentorship and relationships with him JESUS. If you desire to be mentored in the prophetic calling and ministry, contact us by writing and requesting for materials. We will help you find your prophetic mentor, and or will give prophetic counseling, to get you equip to find your true prophetic mentor.

NOTES:

NOTES:

APFM ~ ASSESSMENT FORM

First Name: _____

Last Name: _____

Have you Identified the call on your life: ( ) Yes   ( ) No

If yes please specify:

_____

When did you identify that call?

_____

What have you experienced in taking this course?

_____

Was the information from the course what you expected to receive? ( ) Yes   ( ) No
If yes please specify:

_____

Is there anything that you would like to see added to our courses?

_____

How will you apply the course related information to the next level of ministry in your life?

_____

Are you looking for more direct information and mentoring please specify:

_____

APFM ~ Enrollment Form

First Name: _____ Last Name: _____

Address: _____

Home Ph.: _____ Cell Ph.: _____

Email: _____ Web: _____

Church Affiliation: _____

Name of Pastor(s) _____

Church Address: _____ Ph.: _____

Have you identified the call on your life   ( ) Yes   ( ) No

If yes please specify: _____

How did you hear about A Prophetic Flow Ministries Inc.?
( ) Flyer   ( ) Church   ( ) Friend   ( ) Email   ( ) Other

Class	Description	Class	Description
Part 1	Dreams & Visions	Part 2	Revelation/dreams & Vision for the Church
Part 3	Birthing the prophet	Part 4	Advanced prophetic education/fulfilling a mandate
Part 5	Unveiling the end time kingdom church		

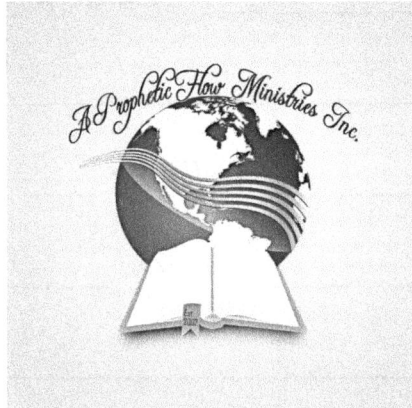

If you would like to have APFM come to your church and do classes or a seminar contact us at.

Facebook.com/ Email:
 kingdomadvanceministries8@yahoo.com
propheticflowministries@yahoo.com
flowinprophet@gmail.com

Reach us by web:
www.kingdomadvancementministries.vpweb.com

When sending or making payments: Pay Pal: Victoria L. Woods~ APFM ~ A Prophetic Flow Ministries Inc.

Church office: 609-677-8684
Administrator: 609-328-0390
Personal Assistant: 609-335-8351

ABOUT THE AUTHOR

Prophetess Victoria L. Woods is the founder and CEO of **A Prophetic Flow Ministries Inc.** which has been in establishment for over 10 years. *She is also the Co ~Pastor of* **Kingdom Advancement Ministries Inc.***, where she and her husband Mark A. Woods Sr.,~ Senior Pastor, are the under-shepherds. She is the mother of three children and one grandchild; Prophetess Victoria L. Woods has a yoke destroying anointing of healing and deliverance that penetrates the kingdom of darkness. She has an "in your face", raw message for the end-time church. God has anointed and appointed Prophetess Woods in this hour to give impartation of truth and to birth out and elevate God's end time prophets.*

A Prophetic Flow Ministries Inc. is a company of prophets that is a fivefold ministry and leadership training school. God has breathed upon the school to birth forth the anointing of the Office Prophet and prophetic people alike. Prophetess Woods has a way of teaching the prophetic to God's people at a level of impregnation where, once touched, they will never be the same again. The fruit of her anointing causes those taught by her to bear much fruit and birth forth ministries. Her mandate is to prophetically reclaim spiritual territories and regions and to awake the sleeping church. Prophetess Woods is a specialist in the Spirit. She was given, in a vision by God, the curriculum to start the school of the prophets to strategically teach, train, and mentor sons and daughters to their correct place and office.

She has a word in her belly to bring back living waters to the church, to get rid of stale and stagnant waters, and to prepare the bride for Jesus Christ's second coming.

www.ingramcontent.com/pod-product-compliance
Lightning Source LLC
Chambersburg PA
CBHW081237090426
42738CB00016B/3338